2ⁿᵈ E

GOLD AHEAD

With Financial Study Guide

THE RICHEST
MAN IN BABYLON

BY GEORGE S. CLASON

Series: Read and Listen by QR Codes

George S. Clason

GOLD AHEAD, A Saga for Practical Treasure Hunters by George S. Clason was first published in 1937 by The Institute of Financial Education, Denver, Colorado. The 2nd Edition of *GOLD AHEAD* was published in 1940 by Financial Education Publishers, Denver, Colorado. Both are in the public domain.

 The original 1940 title for the book commonly known as **The Richest Man in Babylon** was *GOLD AHEAD*. The new title was extracted from the title of Chapter Two – "The Richest Man in Babylon Tells His System".

This book, **The Richest Man in Babylon, 2nd Edition, Gold Ahead with Financial Study Guide**, by George S. Clason, is the unabridged 1940 publication of **Gold Ahead**, with the addition of the powerful 1937 Forward by E. McPherson Cole.

NOTE: Unfortunately, most of the newer versions of *The Richest Man in Babylon* have left out "Part Two" from the original book, *GOLD AHEAD*. Part Two covers, "How to Study for Financial Success," and "How to Analyze Financial Problems."

The good news is you are receiving the full story. You won't miss a single word of wisdom from George S. Clason's book.

SRAAR Partnership
Website: https://MoreHelp.us/C-40
Email: SRAAR@EinsteinThinkers.com
1310 Wilkinson Drive
Plant City, FL, USA 33566

QR Codes sends you to the chapter-by chapter →→→ professional narration by Mr. Steve Hoover.

ISBN: 978-1-959249-04-7

Look for the Series:
Read and Listen by QR Codes

DEDICATION by George S. Clason 1937

To you who desire much gold, this book is dedicated. May you have gold in plenty. May you enjoy it without limit. May posterity be grateful that you lived and enjoyed and made this world a happier place for those who follow.

~ ~ ~ ~ ~ ~ ~

DEDICATION by Stan Reynolds 2022

I dedicate this book to You, the reader. It is your desire to grow intellectually and financially that will ensure your future prosperity. As you apply the principles found within these pages, your bank accounts shall certainly grow, and so will you. You will be truly blessed as you share your blessings with others.

CONTENTS

ACKNOWLEDGMENTS

This book would not have been possible without the support and conscientious efforts of Angela Ardrey-Reynolds. My sincerest appreciation for her commitment to this project and our readers.

Special thanks to our professional narrator Steve Hoover for a stellar performance. His work brings to life each character in vivid clarity. His narration will help you to experience each word just as if you were present in old Babylon, listening to the wisdom of the teachers.

Cover Art by Robert Thiemann and Michael Steinberg.

Cover design by Stanley J. Reynolds.

This 1940 edition, by George S. Clason, is in the public domain. Thanks to The Institute of Financial Education Denver the publisher.

The original, 1937 illustrations by Harry G. Miller and M. S. Harms.

All illustrations were photographed by Stanley J. Reynolds and edited utilizing Adobe's Photoshop version 23.42.

This book has been produced in compliance with copyright law.

TWO FOREWORDS

First Addition 1937 and Second Addition 1940

1940 – Second Edition Foreword
By Financial Education Publishers
https://MoreHelp.us/C-23 →

Our prosperity as a nation depends upon the personal financial prosperity of each of us as individuals.

This book deals with the personal successes of each of us. Success means accomplishments as the result of our own efforts and abilities. Proper preparation is the key to our success. Our acts can be no wiser than our thoughts. Our thinking can be no wiser than our understanding.

GOLD AHEAD has been termed a guide to financial understanding. That, indeed, is its purpose; to offer those who are ambitious for financial success an insight which will aid them to acquire money, to keep money, and to make their surpluses earn more money.

In the pages which follow, the author takes us back to Babylon, the cradle in which was nurtured the basic principles of finance now recognized and used the world over.

To the new readers of *GOLD AHEAD,* the Publishers extend the wish that its pages may contain for them the same inspiration for growing bank accounts, greater financial successes, and the solution of difficult personal financial problems as so enthusiastically reported by readers from coast to coast.

To the business executives who have distributed the book in such generous quantities to friends, relatives, employees, and associates, the Publishers take this opportunity to express their gratitude. No endorsement could be higher than that of practical men who appreciate its teachings because they, themselves, have worked up to important successes by applying the very principle it advocates.

Babylon became the wealthiest city of the ancient world because its citizens were the richest people of their time. They appreciated the value of money. They practiced sound financial principles in acquiring money, keeping money, and making their money earn more money. They provided for themselves what we as individuals all desire, incomes for the future, **"GOLD AHEAD."**

1937 FOREWORD – BY E. MCPHERSON COLE

"GOLD AHEAD"! What thrilling thoughts these two words arouse! *They are our call to action.* Immediately we feel an inner stirring – a desire to be off to distant, mysterious places. This urge to seek and find unlimited treasure has led men to the far corners of the earth and has been an important factor in the civilization of out-of-the-way localities.

This was the call which started the greatest and most successful treasure hunt in all of history. When Columbus returned to Spain from his discovery of America, he had with him pieces of gold bartered from the natives in the West Indies. The natives did not know its source, vaguely telling him it came from the mainland where there was plenty more.

Columbus wanted Queen Isabel to feel that she had been justified in financing his expedition of discovery, so, with flowery speeches he presented his samples to the queen explaining the reports of the natives that the mainland was a country of unlimited gold.

Spain was electrified at his reports. Expedition after expedition was organized and embarked for the new Eldorado. Thousands followed his trail across the ocean, lured on by the thrill of treasure hunting, enduring stoically the same hardships at which the sailors of Columbus had mutinied. And then after landing, going on eagerly to greater dangers and more insufferable hardships.

We can but marvel at the energy and determination of these early Spaniards. They penetrated as far inland as Oklahoma and Colorado. They crossed the continent to California. Finally, in the heart of Mexico and upon the western slopes of the Andes in South America they discovered treasures of gold so tremendous as to be far beyond their greatest hopes. Ruthlessly they took these from their owners, the Aztecs and the Incas, and sent gold back to Spain, actually by the shipload. Thus was the most successful treasure hunt of all time carried to a conclusion.

In later years, the same call spurred on the gold seekers to cross the continent to California, to the gold diggings of Colorado, Idaho, Montana, Nevada, and even across the icy passes to the golden sands of the Klondyke. In other parts of the globe, the same call brought rushes of eager treasure seekers to Canada, New Zealand, the Transvaal and innumerable other localities where golden treasures waited to be claimed.

The virgin treasures of gold no longer sparkle in out-of-the-way stream beds awaiting the coming of the prospector. Those days are over. In his frantic search for the new gold fields, man has fairly well covered the face of the earth. Yet we still have the instincts of the treasure hunters and the urge to seek and find.

At the present time, when it would seem that we are debarred from gratifying our desires to hunt for treasures, there comes to us the dominating character of this book, Arkad – reported, and quite rightly so, to be the richest man in the richest city in the world at the time he lived, Babylon. Arkad, like us, was at heart a treasure seeker. He deeply and sincerely desired to possess much gold. He did not try to deceive himself into thinking what he really wanted were things much finer than gold. He was practical and knew that gold made possible the finer things he might desire. So he set out to get gold, enough of it to enable him to gratify his own needs and desires with an ample surplus so he could do good in the world.

There were no new gold fields within reach of Babylon to which this ambitious youth could rush and make his pile. He was confronted with the problem of getting his start from a most humble beginning and building up his fortune right there in Babylon where jobs paid minimum wages and competition in all sorts of business was just as keen as it has ever been anywhere, before or since. Arkad was a thinker. It never occurred to him to say to himself that it just couldn't be done and he might as well be reconciled to plod along in comparative property like the rest of the young men in his crowd. He knew it could be done if he were just able to find out how.

So he kept on thinking and studying how he could share in the wealth so in evidence among many residents of this wealthy city. The result of his desire coupled with his determination was the discovery of a system that eventually led him to financial success; not just ordinary success but a most abundant success. This system he explains to us. It is just as practical today as it was in those bygone days of ancient Babylon.

The old prospectors of our pioneer mining days, those grizzly veterans of much experience, had an expression they aptly used when gold was discovered in some new formation or some locality where according to geology or experiences it should not exist. They would say, *"Gold is where you find it"*. Arkad shows us that an abundance of gold can and probably does exist in places where we would not think to look for it, places quite within our reach without any need of our rushing off to distant diggings where we may or may not find it. We can forego the thirsty deserts, the icy mountains and the fever-infested tropical swamps and do our treasure hunting in much more congenial surroundings. He offers us a broad highway that will lead us safely and surely to the treasures we desire to find if we but have in us the instincts of true treasure hunters and the willingness to endure, as those old timers endured, the privations and the labors that must be surmounted before we can claim that **"Gold Ahead"** we sincerely desire.

Moreover, he shows us that the rewards of treasure hunting by his system are fully as great as when men rushed to distant gold fields, while the privations and hardships are certainly no more difficult. Success is waiting for those who have the will power to go and get it. However, we must not get an erroneous impression that success is reserved for super men and women. Such is not the case at all. We do not need to be a super man to have will power. Will power is something we can all have and use. Lest there be a mistaken conception of will power, let me quote an apt definition from Arkad's own words:

"Do not think will power gives a man the strength to lift a burden the camel cannot carry, or to draw a load the oxen cannot budge. Will power is but the unflinching purpose to carry a task you set for yourself to fulfillment. If I set for myself a task, be it ever so trifling, I shall see it through. How else shall I have confidence in myself to do important things?"

In this bit of wisdom, Arkad has given us one of the cardinal principles to financial success, the idea of carrying through to our ultimate goal. It was certainly necessary for the treasure seekers of old. The laggers and the quitters never brought home their bags filled with gold.

In writing the foreword to this book containing Mr. Clason's tales of the wise, rich men of old Babylon, I do so with a deep conviction that it is destined to take its place among that small group of classics that live on and on because they have a message of inherent value to men of all time. Herein is a message of financial abundance, a broad road through this land of plenty which all can follow if they but have the intelligence and the desire. Nature is lavish with her riches. She does not count the blades of grass or limit the number of leaves on the tree. She is equally liberal with the good things of life. They are here in abundance for those who will prepare themselves to share the plentiful supply.

My conviction of a long and useful career for this book is based upon the fact that it offers help to every individual in solving his own, personal financial problems with wisdom and that, still more important, it teaches in a clear, interesting, and never-to-be-forgotten manner a true understanding of the principles underlying permanent financial success. It offers definite help to those wrestling with financial difficulties beyond their training. It supplies an understanding that will prove of the utmost value to that vast army of young folks who yearly leave our schools and colleges to make their way in this world where knowledge of money is so essential to their future usefulness and happiness.

It has been my privilege to read many of the letters of approval on these tales of Babylon which are constantly coming to their author. Some are from the younger folks who have found in them just the wise guidance they need. By far the large number are from seasoned personalities whose long years of experience in finance and business give them a fine sense of appreciation for real merit. To them the tales recall their own experiences, their long hard struggles to achieve success and often their costly financial mistakes; mistakes that could have been so easily avoided, had their vision been clearer or their experience more extensive. I am going to quote from one of these letters written by a gentleman in Indiana. He had learned his financial wisdom, as can be easily recognized from his letter, in the bitter and expensive school of experience. Here is the way he expresses his appreciation of the wisdom of The Richest Man in Babylon:

"I only wish I could have had access to his wisdom during my younger years. It would have saved me from so many costly and unnecessary financial mistakes. It would have helped make my successes so much greater. That my children may have full benefit of this wisdom when they are old enough to understand, I am now putting aside separate copies for each of them."

This gentleman expresses my own feeling and I consider it a privilege to add that I hope all the young folks of the coming generations may share with his children the opportunity to know and use to their own financial advancement the wisdom of THE RICHEST MAN IN BABYLON.

Any effort on my part to convey to the reader the contents of the following pages or to urge them to read and use them would be futile. The masterly touch of the author needs no explanation or commendation.

To every person ambitious for greater financial success and to all who desire to lead that fuller, richer life that financial success makes available, I recommend that they read this book.

Let us all be treasure hunters! There is **GOLD AHEAD** waiting to be claimed - plenty of it. We can all be successful treasure hunters! Let us be on our way!

> *GOLD is the medium by which earthly success is measured.*

> *GOLD makes possible the enjoyment of the best the earth affords.*

> *GOLD is plentiful for those who understand the simple laws that govern its acquisition.*

> *GOLD is governed today by the same laws that controlled it when men thronged the streets of Babylon six thousand years ago.*

Part 1

"We are weary of being without gold in the midst of plenty."

"Why cannot we have our share of the good things so plentiful for those who have the gold to buy them?"

CHAPTER I

THE TELL OF THE MAN
WHO DESIRED MUCH GOLD

Bansir, the chariot builder of Babylon, was thoroughly discouraged. From his seat upon the low wall surrounding his property, he gazed sadly at his simple home and the open workshop in which stood a partially completed chariot.

Listen to Audio

https://MoreHelp.us/C-1 →

His wife frequently appeared at the open door. Her furtive glances in his direction reminded him that the meal bag was almost empty, and he should be at work finishing the chariot, hammering and hewing, polishing and painting, stretching taut the leather over the wheel rims, preparing it for delivery so he could collect from his wealthy customer.

Nevertheless, his fat, muscular body sat stolidly upon the wall. His slow mind was struggling patiently with a problem for which he could find no answer. The hot, tropical sun, so typical of this valley of the Euphrates, beat down upon him mercilessly. Beads of perspiration formed upon his brow and trickled down unnoticed to lose themselves in the hairy jungle on his chest.

Beyond his home towered the high terraced walls surrounding the king's palace. Nearby, cleaving the blue heavens, was the painted tower to the Temple of Bel. In the shadow of such grandeur was his simple home and many others far less neat and well cared for. Babylon was like this—a mixture of grandeur and squalor, of dazzling wealth and direst poverty, crowded together without plan or system within the protecting walls of the city.

Behind him, had he cared to turn and look, the noisy chariots of the rich, jostled and crowded aside the sandaled tradesmen as well as the barefooted beggars. Even the rich, in turn, were forced to turn into the gutters to clear the way for the long lines of slave water carriers, on the "King's Business", each bearing a heavy goatskin of water to be poured upon the hanging gardens.

Bansir was too engrossed in his own problem to hear or heed the confused hubbub of the busy city. It was the unexpected twanging of the strings from a familiar lyre that aroused him from his reverie. He turned and looked into the sensitive, smiling face of his best friend—Kobbi, the musician.

"May the Gods bless thee with great liberality, my good friend," began Kobbi with an elaborate salute. "Yet, it does appear they have already been so generous, thou neediest not to labor. I rejoice with thee in thy good fortune. More, I would even share it with thee. Pray, from thy purse which must be bulging, else thou wouldst be busy in yon shop, extract but two humble shekels and lend them to me until after the noblemen's feast this night. Thou wilt not miss them ere they are returned."

"If I did have two shekels," Bansir responded gloomily, "to no one could I lend them—not even to you, my best of friends; for they would be my fortune—my entire fortune. No one lends his entire fortune, not even to his best friend."

"What!" exclaimed Kobbi with genuine surprise, "Thou hast not one shekel in thy purse, yet sit like a statue upon a wall! Why not complete that chariot? How else canst thou provide for thy noble appetite? 'Tis not like thee, my friend. Where is thy endless energy? Doth something distress thee? Have the Gods brought to thee troubles?"

"A torment from the Gods it must be," Bansir agreed. "It began with a dream, a senseless dream, in which I thought I was a man of means. From my belt hung a handsome purse, heavy with coins. There were shekels which I cast with careless freedom to the beggars; there were pieces of silver with which I did buy finery for my wife and whatever I did desire for myself; there were pieces of gold which made me feel assured of the future and unafraid to spend the silver. A glorious feeling of contentment was within me! You would not have known me for thy hard-working friend. Nor wouldst have known my wife, so free from wrinkles was her face, and shining with happiness. She was again the smiling maiden of our early married days."

"A pleasant dream, indeed," commented Kobbi, "but why should such pleasant feelings as it aroused turn thee into a glum statue upon the wall?"

"Why, indeed! Because when I awoke and remembered how empty was my purse, a feeling of rebellion swept over me. Let us talk it over together, for, as the sailors do say, we ride in the same boat, we two. As youngsters, we went together to the priests to learn wisdom. As young men, we shared each other's pleasures. As grown men, we have always been close friends. We have been contented subjects of our king. We have been satisfied to work long hours and spend our earnings freely. We have earned much coin in the years that have passed, yet to know the joys that come from wealth, we must dream about them. Bah! Are we more than dumb sheep? We live in the richest city in all the world. The travelers do say none equals it in wealth. About us is much display of wealth, but of it we ourselves have naught. After half a lifetime of hard labor, thou, my best of friends, has an empty purse and sayest to me, 'May I borrow such a trifle as two shekels until after the noblemen's feast this night?' Then, what do I reply? Do I say, 'Here is my purse; its contents will I gladly share?' No, I admit that my purse is as empty as thine. What is the matter? Why cannot we acquire silver and gold—more than enough for food and robes?

"Consider, also, our sons," Bansir continued, "are they not following in the footsteps of their fathers? Need they and their families and their sons and their sons' families live all their lives in the midst of such treasures of gold, and yet, like us, be content to banquet upon sour goat's milk and porridge?"

"Never, in all the years of our friendship, didst talk like this before, Bansir." Kobbi was puzzled.

"Never in all those years did I think like this before. From early dawn until darkness stopped me, I have labored to build the finest chariots any man could make, soft-heartedly hoping someday the Gods would recognize my worthy deeds and bestow upon me great prosperity. This they have never done. At last, I realize this they will never do. Therefore, my heart is sad. I wish to be a man of means. I wish to own lands and cattle, to have fine robes and coins in my purse. I am willing to work for these things with all the strength in my back, with all the skill in my hands, with all the cunning in my mind, but I wish my labors to be fairly rewarded. What is the matter with us? Again, I ask you! Why cannot we have our just share of the good things so plentiful for those who have the gold with which to buy them?"

"Would I knew an answer!" Kobbi replied. "No better than thou am I satisfied. My earnings from my lyre are quickly gone. Often must I plan and scheme that my family be not hungry. Also, within my breast is a deep longing for a lyre large enough that it may truly sing the strains of music that do surge through my mind. With such an instrument could I make music finer than even the king has heard before."

"Such a lyre thou shouldst have. No man in all Babylon could make it sing more sweetly; could make it sing so sweetly, not only the king but the Gods themselves would be delighted. But how mayest thou secure it while we both of us are as poor as the king's slaves. Listen to the bell! Here they come." He pointed to the long column of half-naked, sweating water bearers plodding laboriously up the narrow street from the river. Five abreast they marched, each bent under a heavy goatskin of water.

"A fine figure of a man, he who doth lead them." Kobbi indicated the wearer of the bell who marched in front without a load. "A prominent man in his own country, 'tis easy to see."

"There are many good figures in the line," Bansir agreed, "as good men as we. Tall, blond men from the north, laughing black men from the south, little brown men from the nearer countries. All marching together from the river to the gardens, back and forth, day after day, year after year. Naught of happiness to look forward to. Beds of straw upon which to sleep—hard grain porridge to eat. Pity the poor brutes, Kobbi!"

"Pity them I do. Yet, thou dost make me see how little better off are we, free men though we call ourselves."

"That is truth, Kobbi, unpleasant thought, though it be. We do not wish to go on year after year living slavish lives. Working, working, working! Getting nowhere."

"Might we not find out how others acquire gold and do as they do?" Kobbi inquired.

"Perhaps there is some secret we might learn if we but sought from those who knew," replied Bansir thoughtfully.

"This very day," suggested Kobbi, "I did pass our old friend, Arkad, riding in his golden chariot. This, I will say, he did not look over my humble head as many in his station might consider his right. Instead, he did wave his hand that all onlookers might see him pay greetings and bestow his smile of friendship upon Kobbi, the musician."

"He is claimed to be the richest man in all Babylon," Bansir mused.

"So rich, the king is said to seek his golden aid in affairs of the treasury," Kobbi replied.

"So rich," Bansir interrupted, "I fear if I should meet him in the darkness of the night, I should lay my hands upon his fat wallet."

"Nonsense," reproved Kobbi, "a man's wealth is not in the purse he carries. A fat purse quickly empties if there be no golden stream to refill it. Arkad has an income that constantly keeps his purse full, no matter how liberally he spends."

"Income, that is the thing," ejaculated Bansir: "I wish an income that will keep flowing into my purse whether I sit upon the wall or travel to far lands. Arkad must know how a man can make an income for himself. Dost suppose it is something he could make clear to a mind as slow as mine?"

"Methinks, he did teach his knowledge to his son, Nomasir," Kobbi responded. "Did he not go to Nineveh and, so it is told at the inn, become without aid from his father, one of the richest men in that

8

city?"

"Kobbi, thou bringest to me a rare thought." A new light gleamed in Bansir's eyes. "It costs nothing to ask wise advice from a good friend, and Arkad was always that. Never mind though our purses be as empty as the falcon's nest of a year ago. Let that not detain us. We are weary of being without gold in the midst of plenty. We wish to become men of means. Come, let us go to Arkad and ask how we, also, may acquire incomes for ourselves."

"Thou speakest with true inspiration, Bansir. Thou bringeth to my mind a new understanding. Thou makest me to realize the reason why we have never found any measure of wealth. We never sought it. Thou labored patiently to build the staunchest chariots in Babylon. To that purpose was devoted your best endeavors. Therefore, at it, thou didst succeed. I strove to become a skillful lyre player. And, at it, I did succeed.

"In those things toward which we exerted our best endeavors we succeeded. The Gods were content to let us continue thus. Now, at last, we see a light bright like that from the rising sun. It biddeth us to learn more that we may prosper more. 'Tis the wisest thing we have ever done. With a new understanding, we shall find honorable ways to accomplish our desires."

"Let us go to Arkad this very day," Bansir urged. "Also, let us ask other friends of our boyhood days, who have fared no better than ourselves, to join us that they, too, may share in his wisdom."

"Thou wert ever thus thoughtful of thy friends, Bansir. Therefore, hast thou many friends. It shall be as thou sayest. We go this day and take them with us."

CHAPTER II

THE RICHEST MAN IN BABYLON
TELLS HIS SYSTEM

If you have not acquired more than a bare existence since we were youths, it is because you either have failed to learn the laws that govern the building of wealth, or else you do not observe them.

The Richest Man in Babylon Tells His System

In old Babylon, there once lived a certain very rich man named Arkad. Far and wide he was famed for his great wealth. Also was he famed for his liberality. He was generous in his charities. He was generous with his family. He was liberal in his own expenses. But nevertheless, each year his wealth increased more rapidly than he spent it.

Listen to Audio

https://MoreHelp.us/C-2 →

And there were certain friends of younger days who came to him and said: "You, Arkad, are more fortunate than we. You have become the richest man in all of Babylon while we struggle for existence. You can wear the finest garments and you can enjoy the rarest foods, while we must be content if we can clothe our families in raiment that is presentable and feed them as best, we can.

"Yet, once we were equal. We studied under the same master. We played in the same games. And in neither the studies nor the games did you outshine us. And in the years since, you have been no more an honorable citizen than we.

"Nor, have you worked harder or more faithfully, in so far as we can judge. Why, then, should a fickle fate single you out to enjoy all the good things of life and ignore us who are equally deserving?"

Thereupon Arkad remonstrated with them, saying, "If you have not acquired more than a bare existence in the years since we were youths, it is because you either have failed to learn the laws that govern the building of wealth, or else you do not observe them.

"'Fickle fate' is a vicious goddess that brings no permanent good to anyone. On the contrary, she brings ruin to almost every man upon whom she showers unearned gold. She makes wanton spenders, who soon dissipate all they receive and are left beset by overwhelming appetites and desires they have not the ability to gratify. Yet others whom she favors become misers and hoard their wealth, fearing to spend what they have, knowing they do not possess the ability to replace it. They further are beset by fear of robbers and doom themselves to lives of emptiness and secret misery.

One may sail the distant seas.

"Others, there probably are, who can take unearned gold and add to it, and continue to be happy and contented citizens. But so few are they, I know of them, but by hearsay. Think you of the men who have inherited sudden wealth, and see if these things are not so.
His friends admitted that of the men they knew who had inherited wealth these words were true, and they besought him to explain to them how he had become possessed of so much property, so he continued:

"In my youth I looked about me and saw all the good things there were to bring happiness and contentment. And I realized that wealth increased the potency of all these.

"Wealth is a power. With wealth many things are possible.

"One may ornament the home with the richest of furnishings.

"One may sail the distant seas.

"One may feast on the delicacies of far lands.

"One may buy the ornaments of the gold worker and the stone polisher.

"One may even build mighty temples for the Gods.

"One may do all these things and many others in which there is delight for the senses and gratification for the soul." And when I realized all this, I declared to myself that I would claim my share of the good things of life. I would not be one of those who stand afar off, enviously watching others enjoy. I would not be content to clothe myself in the cheapest raiment that looked respectable. I would not be satisfied with the lot of a poor man. On the contrary, I would make myself a guest at this banquet of good things.

"Being, as you know, the son of a humble merchant, one of a large family with no hope of an inheritance, and not being endowed, as you have so frankly said, with superior powers or wisdom, I decided that if I was to achieve what I desired, time and study would be required.

"As for time, all men have it in abundance. You, each of you, have let slip by sufficient to have made yourselves wealthy. Yet, you admit you have nothing to show except your good families, of which you can be justly proud.

"As for study, did not our wise teacher teach us that learning was of two kinds: the one kind being the things we learned and knew, and the other being in the training that taught us how to find out what we did not know?

"Therefore, did I decide to find out how one might accumulate wealth, and when I had found out, to make this my task and do it well. For, is it not wise that we should enjoy while we dwell in the brightness of the sunshine, for sorrows enough shall descend upon us when we depart for the darkness of the world of spirit?

"I found employment as a scribe in the hall of records, and long hours each day I labored upon the clay tablets. Week after week, and month after month, I labored, yet for my earnings I had naught to show. Food and clothing and penance to the gods, and other things of which I could remember not what, absorbed all my earnings. But my determination did not leave me.

"And one day Algamish, the money lender, came to the house of the city master and ordered a copy of the Ninth Law, and he said to me, 'I must have this in two days, and if the task is done by that time, two coppers will I give to thee.'

"So I labored hard, but the law was long, and when Algamish returned, the task was unfinished. He was angry, and had I been his slave, he would have beaten me. But knowing the city master would not permit him to injure me, I was unafraid, so I said to him: " 'Algamish, you are a very rich man. Tell me how I may also become rich, and all night I will carve upon the clay, and when the sun rises.

It shall be completed.' He smiled at me and replied, 'You are a forward knave, but we will call it a bargain.

"All that night I carved, though my back pained and the smell of the wick made my head ache until my eyes could hardly see. But when he returned at sunup, the tablets were complete.

14

" 'Now,' I said, 'tell me what you promised.'

" 'You have fulfilled your part of our bargain, my son,' he said to me kindly, 'and I am ready to fulfill mine. I will tell you these things you wish to know because I am becoming an old man, and an old tongue loves to wag. And when youth comes to age for advice, he receives the wisdom of years. But too often does youth think that age knows only the wisdom of days that are gone, and therefore profits not. But remember this, the sun that shines today is the sun that shone when thy father was born, and will still be shining when thy last grandchild shall pass into the darkness.

"' The thoughts of youth,' he continued, 'are bright things that shine forth like the meteors that oft make brilliant the sky, but the wisdom of age is like the fixed stars that shine so unchanged that the sailor may depend upon them to steer his course.

" 'Mark you well my words, for if you do not you will fail to grasp the truth that I will tell you, and you will think that your night's work has been in vain.'

One may feast on the delicacies of far lands.

"Then he looked at me shrewdly from under his shaggy brows and said in a low, forceful tone, 'I found the road to wealth when I decided that a part of all I earned was mine to keep. And so will you.'

"Then he continued to look at me with a glance that I could feel pierce me but said no more.

" 'Is that all?" I asked.

" 'That was sufficient to change the heart of a sheep herder into the heart of a money lender,' he replied.

" 'But all I earn is mine to keep, is it not?' I demanded.

" 'Far from it,' he replied. 'Do you not pay the garment-maker? Do you not pay the sandal-maker? Do you not pay for the things you eat? Can you live in Babylon without spending? What have you to show for your earnings of the past month? What for the past year? Fool! You pay to everyone but yourself. Dullard, you labor for others. As well be a slave and work for what your master gives you to eat and wear. If you did keep for yourself one-tenth of all you earn, how much would you have in ten years?'

"My knowledge of the numbers did not forsake me, and I answered, 'As much as I earn in one year.'

" 'You speak but half the truth,' he retorted. 'Every gold piece you save is a slave to work for you. Every copper it earns is its child that also can earn for you. If you would become wealthy, then what you save must earn, and its children must earn, and its children's children must earn, that all may help to give to you the abundance you crave.

" 'You think I cheat you for your long night's work,' he continued, 'but I am paying you a thousand times over if you have the intelligence to grasp the truth I offer you.

"'A PART OF ALL YOU EARN IS YOURS TO KEEP. It should not be less than a tenth no matter how little you earn. It can be as much more as you can afford. Pay yourself first. Do not buy from the clothes-maker and the sandal-maker more than you can pay out of the rest and still have enough for food and charity and penance to the gods.

" 'Wealth, like a tree, grows from a tiny seed. The first copper you save is the seed from which your tree of wealth shall grow. The sooner you plant that seed, the sooner shall the tree grow. And the more faithfully you nourish and water that tree with consistent savings, the sooner may you bask in contentment beneath its shade.' So saying, he took his tablets and went away.

"I thought much about what he had said to me, and it seemed reasonable. So I decided that I would try it. Each time I was paid, I took one from each ten pieces of copper and hid it away. And strange as it may seem, I was no shorter of funds than before. I noticed little difference as I managed to get along without it. But often I was tempted as my hoard began to grow, to spend it for some of the good things the merchants displayed, brought by camels and ships from the land of the Phoenicians. But I wisely refrained.

"A twelfth month after Algamish had gone, he again returned and said to me, 'Son, have you paid to yourself not less than one-tenth of all you have earned for the past year?'

"I answered proudly, 'Yes, master, I have.'

" That is good,' he answered beaming upon me, 'And what have you done with it?'
" 'I have given it to Azmur, the brickmaker, who told me he was traveling over the seven seas and in Tyre he would buy for me the

rare jewels of the Phoenicians. When he returns, we shall sell these at high prices and divide the earnings.'

" 'Every fool must learn,' he growled, 'but why trust the knowledge of a brickmaker about jewels? Would you go to the bread maker to inquire about the stars? No, by my tunic, you would go to the astrologer, if you had power to think. Your savings are gone, youth, you have jerked your wealth tree up by the roots. But plant another. Try again. And next time if you would have advice about jewels, go to the jewel merchant. If you would know the truth about sheep, go to the herdsman. Advice is one thing that is freely given away, but watch that you take only what is worth having. He who takes advice about his savings from one who is inexperienced in such matters, shall pay with his savings for proving the falsity of their opinions.' Saying this, he went away.

"And it was as he said. For the Phoenicians are scoundrels and sold to Azmur worthless bits of glass that looked like gems. But as Algamish had bid me, I again saved each tenth copper, for I now had formed the habit and it was no longer difficult.

One may buy ornaments of the gold worker
and the stone polisher.

"A twelve months later, Algamish again came to the room of the scribes and addressed me. 'What progress have you made since last I saw you?'

" 'I have paid myself faithfully,' I replied, 'and my savings I have entrusted to Agger the shield-maker, to buy bronze, and each fourth month he does pay me the rental.'

" That is good. And what do you do with the rental?

" 'I do have a great feast with honey and fine wine and spiced cake. Also, I have bought me a scarlet tunic. And some day I shall buy me a young ass upon which to ride."

"To which Algamish laughed. 'You do eat the children of your savings. Then how do you expect them to work for you? And how can they have children that will also work for you? First get thee an army of golden slaves, and then many a rich banquet may you enjoy without regret.' So saying he again went away.

"Nor did I again see him for two years, when he once more returned and his face was full of deep lines and his eyes drooped, for he was becoming a very old man. And he said to me, 'Arkad, hast thou yet achieved the wealth thou dreamed of?'

"And I answered, 'Not yet all that I desire, but some I have and it earns more, and its earnings earn more.'

" 'And do you still take the advice of brickmakers?'

" 'About brickmaking they give good advice,' I retorted.

" 'Arkad,' he continued, 'you have learned your lessons well. You first learned to live upon less than you could earn. Next, you learned to seek advice from those who were competent through their own experiences to give it. And, lastly, you have learned to make gold work for you.

" 'You have taught yourself how to acquire money, how to keep it, and how to use it. Therefore, you are competent for a responsible position. I am becoming an old man, my sons think only of spending and give no thought to earning. My interests are great and I fear too much for me to look after. If you will go to Nippur and look after my lands there, I shall make you my partner and you shall share in my estate.'

"So I went to Nippur and took charge of his holdings, which were large. And because I was full of ambition, and because I had mastered the three laws of successfully handling wealth, I was enabled to increase greatly the value of his properties. So I prospered much, and when the spirit of Algamish departed for the sphere of darkness, I did share in his estate as he had arranged under the law."

So spoke Arkad, and when he had finished his tale, one of his friends said, "You were indeed fortunate that Algamish made of you an heir."

"Fortunate only in that I had the desire to prosper before I first met him. For four years did I not prove my definiteness of purpose by keeping one-tenth of all I earned? Would you call a fisherman lucky who for years so studied the habits of the fish that with each changing wind he could cast his nets about them? Opportunity is a haughty goddess who wastes no time with those who are unprepared."

"You had strong willpower to keep on after you lost your first year's savings. You are unusual in that way," spoke up another.

"Willpower!" retorted Arkad. "What nonsense. Do you think willpower gives a man the strength to lift a burden the camel cannot carry, or to draw a load the oxen cannot budge? **Willpower is but the unflinching purpose to carry a task you set for yourself to fulfillment.** If I set for myself a task, be it ever so trifling, I shall see it through. How else shall I have confidence in myself to do important things? Should I say to myself, 'For a hundred days as I walk across the bridge into the city, I will pick from the road a pebble and cast it into the stream,' I would do it. If on the seventh day I passed by without remembering, I would not say to myself, 'Tomorrow I will cast two pebbles which will do as well.' Instead, I would retrace my steps and cast the pebble. Nor on the twentieth day would I say to myself, 'Arkad, this is useless. What does it avail you to cast a pebble every day? Throw in a handful and be done with it.' No, I would not say that nor do it. When I set a task for myself, I complete it. Therefore, I am careful not to start difficult and impractical tasks, because I love leisure."

And then another friend spoke up and said, "If what you tell is true, and it does seem as you have said, reasonable, then being so simple, if all men did it, there would not be enough wealth to go around."

One may even build mighty temples for the Gods.

"Wealth grows wherever men exert energy," Arkad replied. "If a rich man builds him a new palace, is the gold he pays out gone? No, the brickmaker has part of it and the laborer has part of it, and the artist has part of it. And everyone who labors upon the house has part of it. Yet when the palace is completed, is it not worth all it cost? And is the ground upon which it stands not worth more because it is there? And is the ground that adjoins it not worth more because it is there? Wealth grows in magic ways. No man can prophesy the limit of it. Have not the Phoenicians built great cities on barren coasts with the wealth that comes from their ships of commerce on the seas?"

"What then do you advise us to do that we also may become rich?" asked still another of his friends. "'The years have passed and we are no longer young men and we have nothing put by."

"I advise that you take the wisdom of Algamish and say to yourselves, 'A part of all I earn is mine to keep.' Say it in the morning when you first arise. Say it at noon. Say it at night. Say it each hour of every day. Say it to yourself until the words stand out like letters of fire across the sky.

"Impress yourself with the idea. Fill yourself with the thought. Then take whatever portions seem wise. **Let it be not less than one-tenth and lay it by.** Arrange your other expenditures to do this if necessary. But lay by that portion first. Soon you will realize what a rich feeling it is to have something upon which you alone have claim. As it grows, it will stimulate you. A new joy of life will thrill you. Greater efforts will come to you to earn more. For of your increased earnings, will not the same percentage be also yours to keep?

"Then learn to make your treasure work for you. Make it your slave. Make its children and its children's children work for you.

"Insure an income for thy future. Look thou at the aged and forget not that in the days to come thou also will be numbered among them. Therefore, invest thy treasure with greatest caution that it be not lost.

22

Usurious rates of return are deceitful sirens that sing but to lure the unwary upon the rocks of loss and remorse.

"Provide also that thy family may not want should the Gods call thee to their realms. For such protection it is always possible to make provision with small payments at regular intervals. Therefore, the provident man delays not in expectation of a large sum becoming available for such a wise purpose.

"Counsel with wise men. Seek the advice of men whose daily work is handling money. Let them save you from such an error as I myself made in entrusting my money to the judgment of Azmur, the brickmaker. A small return and a safe one is far more desirable than risk.

"Enjoy life while you are here. Do not overstrain or try to save too much. If one-tenth of all you earn is as much as you can comfortably keep, be content to keep this portion. Live otherwise according to your income, and let not yourself get niggardly and afraid to spend. Life is good, and life is rich with things worthwhile and things to enjoy."

His friends thanked him and went away. Some were silent, because they had no imagination and could not understand. Some were sarcastic, because they thought that one so rich should divide with old friends not so fortunate. But some had in their eyes a new light. They realized that Algamish had come back each time to the room of the scribes because he was watching a man work his way out of darkness into light. When that man had found the light, a place awaited him. No one could fill that place until he had for himself worked out his own understanding; until he was ready for opportunity.

These latter were the ones, who, in the following years frequently revisited Arkad, who received them gladly. He counseled with them and gave them freely of his wisdom as men of broad experience are always glad to do. And he assisted them in so investing their savings that it would bring in a good interest with safety and would neither be lost nor entangled in investments that paid no dividends.

THE TURNING POINT in these men's lives came upon that day when they realized the truth that had come from Algamish to Arkad and from Arkad to them.

A Part of All Earnings is Yours to Keep!

CHAPTER III

SEVEN REMEDIES FOR A LEAN PURSE

Royal Proclamation

ROYAL PROCLAMATION
THAT ALL MEN MAY HAVE WEALTH.
Heed Ye, Heed Ye, My People,
the command of thy King.

Babylon, our beloved city, is the richest in all the world. Of gold it possesses wealth untold.

Because a few of our worthy citizens do know the laws of wealth, they have grown exceedingly rich. Because the many of our citizens do not know the laws of wealth, they remain poor.

Therefore, that all my faithful subjects may learn the

laws of wealth and be able to acquire gold, have I commanded the wisdom of the wealthy to be taught to all my people.

Be it known that I, your King, have set aside seven days to be devoted to the study of the laws of wealth. Upon the seventeenth day of the first moon do I command all my loyal subjects to seek the teachers I have appointed in every part of our city, that each and all may share justly in the rich treasures of Babylon.

**Heed Ye, Heed Ye, My People,
the command of thy King.**

SARGON, King of Babylon

Tell me, Arkad, "is there any secret to
acquiring wealth? Can it be taught?"

Chapter III

THE TALE OF SEVEN REMEDIES FOR A LEAN PURSE

The glory of Babylon endures. Down through the ages its reputation comes to us as the richest of cities, its treasures as fabulous.

Yet it was not always so. The riches of Babylon were the results of the money wisdom of its people. They first had to learn how to become wealthy.

Listen to Audio

https://MoreHelp.us/C-3 →

When the Good King, SARGON, returned to Babylon after defeating his enemies, the Elamites, he was confronted with a serious situation. The royal Chancellor explained it to the King thus: "After many years of great prosperity brought to our people because your majesty built the great irrigation canals and the mighty temples to the Gods, now that these works are completed, the people seem unable to support themselves.

"The laborers are without employment. The merchants have few customers. The farmers are unable to sell their produce. The people have not enough gold to buy food."

"But where has all the gold gone that we spent for these great improvements?" demanded the King. "It has found its way, I fear," responded the Chancellor, "into the possession of a few very rich men of our city. It filtered through the fingers of most of our people as quickly as the goat's milk goes through the strainer. Now that the stream of gold has ceased to flow, most of our people have nothing to show for their earnings."

The King was thoughtful for some time. Then he asked, "Why should so few men be able to acquire all the gold?"

"Because they know how," replied the Chancellor. "One may not condemn a man for succeeding because he knows how. Neither may one with justice take away from a man what he has fairly earned, to give to men of less ability."

"But why," demanded the King, "should not all the people learn how to accumulate gold and therefore become themselves rich and prosperous?"

"Quite possible, your excellency. But who can teach them? Certainly not the priests, because they know naught of money making."

"Who knows best in all our city how to become wealthy, Chancellor?" asked the King.

"Thy question answers itself, your majesty. Who has amassed the greatest wealth in Babylon?"

"Well said, my able Chancellor. It is Arkad. He is the richest man in Babylon. Bring him before me on the morrow."

Upon the following day, as the King had decreed, Arkad appeared before him, straight and sprightly despite his three score years and ten.

"Arkad," spoke the King, "is it true thou art the richest man in Babylon?"

"So it is reported, your majesty, and no man disputes it."

"How becamest thou so wealthy?"

"By taking advantage of opportunities available to all citizens of our good city."

"Thou hadst nothing to start with?"

"Only a great desire for wealth. Besides this, nothing."

"Arkad," continued the King, "our city is in a very unhappy state because a few men know how to acquire wealth and therefore monopolize it, while the mass of our citizens lack the knowledge of how to keep any part of the gold they receive.

"It is my desire that Babylon be the wealthiest city in the world. Therefore, it must be a city of many wealthy men. Therefore, we must teach all the people how to acquire riches. Tell me, Arkad, is there any secret to acquiring wealth. Can it be taught?"

"It is practical, your majesty. That which one man knows can be taught to others."

The king's eyes glowed. "Arkad, thou speaketh the words I wish to hear. Wilt thou lend thyself to this great cause? Wilt thou teach thy knowledge to a school for teachers, each of whom shall teach others until there are enough trained to teach these truths to every worthy subject in my domain?"

Arkad bowed and said, "I am thy humble servant to command. Whatever of knowledge I possess will I gladly give for the betterment of my fellowmen and the glory of my King. Let your good chancellor arrange for me a class of one hundred men, and I will teach to them those Seven Remedies which did fatten my purse, than which there was none leaner in all Babylon."

A fortnight later, in compliance with the King's command, the chosen hundred assembled in the great hall of the Temple of Learning, seated upon colorful rugs in a semi-circle. Arkad sat beside a small taboret upon which smoked a sacred lamp sending forth a strange and pleasing odor.

"Behold the richest man in Babylon," whispered a student, nudging his neighbor as Arkad arose. "He is but a man even as the rest of us."

"As a dutiful subject of our great King," Arkad began, "I stand before you in his service. Because once I was a poor youth who did greatly desire gold, and because I found knowledge that enabled me to acquire it, he asks that I impart unto you my knowledge.

"I started my fortune in the humblest way. I had no advantage not enjoyed as fully by you and every citizen of Babylon.

"The first storehouse of my treasure was a well-worn purse. I loathed its useless emptiness. I desired that it be round and full, clinking with the sound of gold. Therefore, I sought every remedy for a lean purse. I found seven.

"To you, who are assembled before me, shall I explain the 'Seven Remedies for a Lean Purse' which I do recommend to all men who desire much gold. Each day for seven days will I explain to you one of the Seven Remedies.

"Listen attentively to the knowledge that I will impart. Debate it with me. Discuss it among yourselves. Learn these lessons thoroughly, that ye may also plant in your own purses the seed of wealth. First must each of you start wisely to build a fortune of his own. Then wilt thou be competent, and only then, to teach these truths to others.

"I shall teach to you in simple ways how to fatten your purses. This is the first step leading to the temple of wealth, and no man may climb who cannot plant his feet firmly upon the first step.

"We shall now consider the First Remedy"

THE FIRST REMEDY

Start thy Purse to Fattening

Arkad addressed a thoughtful man in the second row. "My good friend, at what craft workest thou?"

"I," replied the man, "am a scribe and carve records upon the clay tablets."

"Even at such labor did I myself earn my first coppers. Therefore, thou hast the same opportunity to build a fortune."

He spoke to a florid-faced man, farther back. "Pray tell also what dost thou to earn thy bread."

"I," responded this man, "am a meat butcher. I do buy the goats the farmers raise and kill them and sell the meat to the housewives and the hides to the sandal makers."

"Because thou dost also labor and earn, thou hast every advantage to succeed that I did possess."

In this way did Arkad proceed to find out how each man labored to earn his living. When he had done questioning them, he said: "Now, my students, ye can see that there are many trades and labors at which men may earn coins. Each of the ways of earning is a stream of gold from which the worker doth divert by his labors a portion to his own purse. Therefore, into the purse of each of you flows a stream of coins large or small according to his ability. Is it not so?"

Thereupon they agreed that it was so.

"Then," continued Arkad, "if each of you desireth to build for himself a fortune, is it not wise to start by utilizing that source of wealth which he already has established?"

To this they agreed.

The first storehouse of my treasure was a
Well-worn purse. I loathed its emptiness."

Then Arkad turned to a humble man who had declared himself an egg merchant. "If thou select one of thy baskets and put into it each morning ten eggs and take out from it each evening nine eggs, what will eventually happen?"

"It will become in time overflowing."

"Why?"

"Because each day I put in one more egg than I take out."

Arkad turned to the class with a smile. "Does any man here have a lean purse?"

First, they looked amused. Then they laughed. Lastly, they waved their purses in jest.

"All right," he continued, "now I shall tell thee the first remedy I learned to cure a lean purse. Do exactly as I have suggested to the egg merchant. For every ten coins thou placest within thy purse, take out for use but nine. Thy purse will start to fatten at once, and its increasing weight will feel good in thy hand and bring satisfaction to thy soul.

"Deride not what I say because of its simplicity. Truth is always simple. I told thee I would tell how I built my fortune. This was my beginning. I, too, carried a lean purse, and cursed it because there was naught within to satisfy my desires. But when I began to take out from my purse nine parts of ten that I put in, it began to fatten. So will thine!

"Now I will tell a strange truth, the reason for which I know not, when I ceased to pay out more than nine-tenths of my earnings, I managed to get along just as well. I was not shorter than before. Also, ere long, did coins come to me more easily than before. Surely it is a law of the Gods that unto him who keepeth and spendeth not a certain part of all his earnings, shall gold come more easily. Likewise, him whose purse is empty does gold avoid.

> *"This, my students, was the first remedy I did discover for my lean purse: 'For each ten coins I put in, to spend but nine'. Debate this amongst yourselves. If any man proves it untrue, tell me upon the morrow when we shall meet again."*

"Which desirest thou the most? Is it the gratification of thy desires of each day, a jewel, a bit of finery, better raiment, more food; things quickly gone and forgotten? Or is it substantial belongings, gold, lands, herds, merchandise, income bringing investments? The coins thou takest from thy purse bring the first. The coins thou leavest within it will bring the latter.

NOTES: _____

_____

_____

_____

_____

_____

_____

_____

_____

_____

_____

_____

_____

_____

_____

_____

_____

_____

_____

_____

_____

_____

_____

THE SECOND REMEDY

Control thy Expenditures

"Some of your members, my students, have asked me this: 'How can a man keep one-tenth of all he earns in his purse when all the coins he earns are not enough for his necessary expenses?' " So did Arkad address his students upon the second day.

"Yesterday, how many of thee carried lean purses?"

"All of us," answered the class.

"Yet, thou do not all earn the same. Some earn much more than others. Some have much larger families to support. Yet, all purses were equally lean. Now I will tell thee an unusual truth about men and sons of men. It is this: That what each of us calls our 'necessary expenses,' will always grow to equal our incomes, unless we protest to the contrary.

"Confuse not thy necessary expenses with thy desires. Each of you, together with your good families, have more desires than your earnings can gratify. Therefore, are thy earnings spent to gratify these desires insofar as they will go. Still, thou retainest many ungratified desires.

"All men are burdened with more desires than they can gratify. Because of my wealth, thinkest thou, I may gratify every desire? 'Tis a false idea. There are limits to my time. There are limits to my strength. There are limits to the distance I may travel. There are limits to what I may eat. There are limits to the zest with which I may enjoy.

"I say to you that just as weeds grow in a field wherever the farmer leaves space for their roots, even so freely do desires grow in men whenever there is a possibility of their being gratified. Thy desires are a multitude and those that thou mayest gratify are but few.

"Study thoughtfully thy accustomed habits of living. Herein may be most often found certain accepted expenses that may wisely be reduced or eliminated. Let thy motto be one hundred percent of appreciated value demanded for each coin spent.

"Therefore, engrave upon the clay each thing for which thou desireth to spend. Select those that are necessary, and others that are possible through the expenditure of nine-tenths of thy income. Cross out the rest, and consider them but a part of that great multitude of desires that must go unsatisfied, and regret them not.

"Budget then thy necessary expenses. Touch not the one-tenth that is fattening thy purse. Let this be thy great desire that is being fulfilled. Keep working with thy budget, keep adjusting it to help thee. Make it thy first assistant in defending thy fattening purse."

Hereupon one of the students, wearing a robe of red and gold, arose and said, "I am a free man. I believe that it is my right to enjoy the good things of life. Therefore, do I rebel against the slavery of a budget which determines just how much I may spend and for what. I feel it would take much pleasure from my life and make me little more than a pack-ass to carry a burden."

To him Arkad replied. "Who, my friend, would determine thy budget?"

"I would make it for myself," responded the protesting one.

"In that case were a pack-ass to budget his burden, would he include therein jewels and rugs and heavy bars of gold? Not so. He would include hay and grain and a bag of water for the desert trail.

"The purpose of a budget is to help thy purse to fatten. It is to assist thee to have thy necessities and, insofar as attainable, thy other desires. It is to enable thee to realize thy most cherished desires by defending them from thy casual wishes. Like a bright light in a dark cave, thy budget shows up the leaks from thy purse and enables thee to stop them and control thy expenditures for definite and gratifying purposes.

"This then is the Second Remedy for a lean purse. Budget thy expenses that thou mayest have coins to pay for thy necessities, to pay for thy enjoyments, and to gratify thy worthwhile desires without spending more than nine-tenths of thy earnings."

NOTES: _____

_____

_____

_____

_____

_____

_____

_____

_____

_____

_____

_____

_____

_____

_____

_____

_____

_____

_____

THE THIRD REMEDY

Make thy Gold Multiply

"Behold thy lean purse is fattening. Thou hast disciplined thyself to leave therein one-tenth of all thou earneth. Thou hast controlled thy expenditures to protect thy growing treasure. Next, we will consider means to put thy treasure to labor and to increase. Gold in a purse is gratifying to own, and satisfieth a miserly soul, but earns nothing. The gold we may retain from our earnings is but the start. The earnings it will make shall build our fortunes." So spoke Arkad upon the third day to his class.

"How, therefore, may we put our gold to work? My first investment was unfortunate, for I lost all. It's a tale I will relate later. My first profitable investment was a loan I made to a man named Aggar, a shield maker. Once each year, did he buy large shipments of bronze, brought from across the sea to use in his trade. Lacking sufficient capital to pay the merchants, he would borrow from those who had extra coins. He was an honorable man. His borrowing he would repay, together with a liberal rental, as he sold his shields.

"Each time I loaned to him, I loaned back also the rental he had paid to me. Therefore, not only did my capital increase, but its earning likewise increased. Most gratifying was it to have these sums return to my purse.

"I tell you, my students, a man's wealth is not in the coins he carries in his purse; it is the income he buildeth, the golden stream that continually floweth into his purse and keepeth it always bulging. That is what every man desireth. That is what thou, each one of thee, desireth; an income that continueth to come whether thou work or travel.

"Great income I have acquired. So great, that I am called a very rich man. My loans to Aggar were my first training in profitable investment. Gaining wisdom from this experience, I extended my loans and investments as my capital increased. From a few sources at first, from many sources later, flowed into my purse a golden stream of wealth available for such wise uses as I should decide.

"Behold, from my humble earnings, I had begotten a hoard of golden slaves, each laboring and earning more gold. As they labored for me, so their children also labored, and their children's children, until great was the income from their combined efforts.

"Gold increaseth rapidly, when making reasonable earnings as thou wilt see from the following: A farmer, when his first son was born, took ten pieces of silver to a money lender, and asked him to keep it on rental for his son until he became twenty years of age. This the money lender did, and agreed the rental should be one-fourth of its value each four years. The farmer asked, because this sum he had set aside as belonging to his son, that the rental be added to the principal.

"When the boy had reached the age of twenty years, the farmer again went to the money lender to inquire about the silver. The money lender explained that because this sum had been increased by compound interest, the original ten pieces of silver had now grown to thirty and one-half pieces.

"The farmer was well pleased, and because the son did not need the coins, he left them with the money lender. When the son became fifty years of age, the father meantime having passed to the other world, the money lender paid the son in settlement one hundred and sixty-seven pieces of silver.

"Thus in fifty years had the investment multiplied itself at rental almost seventeen times.

"This then is the third remedy for a lean purse, to put each coin to laboring that it may reproduce its kind even as the flocks of the field and help bring to thee income, a stream of wealth that shall flow constantly into thy purse."

NOTES: _____

_____

_____

_____

_____

_____

_____

_____

_____

_____

_____

_____

_____

_____

_____

_____

_____

_____

_____

_____

_____

_____

_____

_____

_____

THE FOURTH REMEDY

Guard thy Treasures from Loss

"Misfortune loves a shining mark. Gold in a man's purse must be guarded with firmness, else it be lost. Thus it is wise that we must first secure small amounts and learn to protect them before the Gods entrust us with larger." So spoke Arkad upon the fourth day to his class.

"Every owner of gold is tempted by opportunities, whereby it would seem that he could make large sums by its investment in most plausible projects. Often friends and relatives are eagerly entering such investment and urge him to follow.

"The first sound principle of investment is security for thy principal. Is it wise to be intrigued by larger earnings when thy principal may be lost? I say not. The penalty of risk is probable loss. Study carefully before parting with thy treasure each assurance, that it may be safely reclaimed. Be not misled by thy own romantic desires to make wealth rapidly.

"Before thou loan it to any man, assure thyself of his ability to repay, and his reputation for doing so, that thou mayest not unwittingly be making him a present of thy hard-earned treasure.

"Before thou entrust it as an investment in any field, acquaint thyself with the dangers which may beset it.

"My own first investment was a tragedy to me at the time. The guarded savings of a year I did entrust to a brickmaker, named Azmur, who was traveling over the far seas, and in Tyre agreed to buy for me the rare jewels of the Phoenicians. These we would sell upon his return and divide the profits. The Phoenicians were

44

scoundrels, and sold him bits of glass. My treasure was lost. Today, my training would show to me at once the folly of entrusting a brickmaker to buy jewels.

"Therefore, do I advise thee from the wisdom of my experiences: be not too confident of thy own wisdom in entrusting thy treasures to the possible pitfalls of investments. Better far consult the wisdom of those experienced in handling money for profit. Such advice is freely given for the asking and may readily possess a value equal in gold to the sum thou considerest investing. In truth such is its actual value, if it save thee from loss.

"This then is the fourth remedy for a lean purse, and of great importance if it prevents thy purse from being emptied once it has become well filled. Guard thy treasure from loss by investing only where thy principal is safe, where it may be reclaimed if desirable, and where thou will not fail to collect a fair rental. Consult with wise men. Secure the advice of men experienced in the profitable handling of gold. Let their wisdom protect thy treasure from unsafe investment."

NOTES: _____

_____

_____

_____

_____

_____

_____

_____

_____

_____

THE FIFTH REMEDY

Make of thy Dwelling a Profitable Investment

"If a man setteth aside nine parts of his earnings upon which to live and enjoy life, and if any part of his nine parts he can turn into a profitable investment without detriment to his wellbeing, then so much faster will his treasures grow." So spoke Arkad, to his class at their fifth lesson.

"All too many of our men of Babylon do raise their families in unseemly quarters. They do pay to exacting landlords liberal rentals for rooms where their wives have not a spot to raise the blooms that gladden a woman's heart and their children have no place to play their games except in the unclean alleys.

"No man's family can fully enjoy life unless they do have a plot of ground wherein children can play in the clean earth, and where the wife may raise not only blossoms, but good rich herbs to feed her family.

'To a man's heart, it brings gladness to eat the figs from his own trees and the grapes of his own vines. To own his own domicile and to have it a place he is proud to care for, putteth confidence in his heart and greater effort behind all his endeavors. Therefore, do I recommend that every man own the roof that sheltereth him and his.

"Nor is it beyond the ability of any well-intentioned man to own his home. Hath not our great king so widely extended the walls of Babylon that within them much land is now unused and may be purchased at sums most reasonable.

"Also I say to you, my students, that the money lenders gladly consider the desires of men who seek homes and lands for their families. Readily may thou borrow to pay the brickmaker and the builder for such commendable purposes, if thou can show a reasonable portion of the necessary sum which thou thyself hath provided for the purpose.

"Then when the house be built, thou canst pay the money lender with the same regularity as thou didst pay the landlord. Because each payment will reduce thy indebtedness to the money lender, a few years will satisfy his loan.

"Then will thy heart be glad because thou wilt own in thy own right a valuable property, and thy only cost will be the king's taxes.

"Also wilt thy good wife go more often to the river to wash thy robes, that each time returning she may bring a goatskin of water to pour upon the growing things.

"Thus come many blessings to the man who owneth his own house. And greatly will it reduce his cost of living, making available more of his earnings for pleasures, and the gratification of his desires."

"This then is the Fifth Remedy for a lean purse. Own thy own home."

NOTES: _____

_____
_____
_____
_____
_____
_____
_____
_____

THE SIXTH REMEDY

Insure a Future Income

"The life of every man proceedeth from his childhood to his old age. This is the path of life, and no man may deviate from it unless the Gods call him prematurely to the world beyond. Therefore, do I say that it behooves a man to make preparation for a suitable income in the days to come, when he is no longer young and to make preparation for his family should he be no longer with them to comfort and support them. This lesson shall instruct thee in providing a full purse when time has made thee less able to earn." So Arkad addressed his class, upon the sixth day.

"The man, who because of his understanding of the laws of wealth, acquired a growing surplus, should give thought to those future days. He should plan certain investments or provisions that may endure safely for many years, yet will be available when the time arrives, which he has so wisely anticipated.

"There are diverse ways by which a man may provide with safety for his future. He may provide a hiding place and there bury a secret treasure. Yet, no matter with what skill it be hidden, it may nevertheless become the loot of thieves. For this reason, I recommend not this plan.

"A man may buy houses or lands for this purpose. If wisely chosen, as to their usefulness and value in the future, they are permanent in their value, and their earnings or their sale will provide well for his purpose.

"A man may loan a small sum to the money lender and increase it at regular periods. The rental which the money lender adds to this will largely add to its increase. I do know a sandal maker, named Ansan, who explained to me not long ago, that each week for eight years, he had deposited with his money lender two pieces of silver. The money lender had but recently given him an accounting over which he greatly rejoiced. The total of his small deposits with their rental, at the customary rate of one-fourth their value for each four years, had now become a thousand and forty pieces of silver.

"I did gladly encourage him further, by demonstrating to him with my knowledge of the numbers, that in twelve years more, if he would keep his regular deposits of but two pieces of silver each week, the money lender would then owe him four thousand pieces of silver, a worthy competence for the rest of his life.

"Surely, when such a small payment, made with regularity, doth produce such profitable results, no man can afford not to insure a treasure for his old age, and the protection of his family, no matter how prosperous his business and his investments may be.

"I would that I might say more about this. In my mind rests a belief, that someday wise thinking men will devise a plan to insure men against death, whereby many men pay in but a trifling sum regularly, the aggregate making a handsome sum for the family of each member who passeth to the beyond. This do I see as something desirable, and which I could highly recommend. But today, it is not possible, because it must reach beyond the life of any man or any partnership to operate. It must be as stable as the King's throne. Someday, do I feel that such a plan shall come to pass, and be a great blessing to many men, because even the first small payment will make available a snug fortune for the family of a member, should he pass on.

"But because we live in our own day and not in the days which are to come, must we take advantage of those means and ways of accomplishing our purposes. Therefore, do I recommend to all men, that they, by wise and well thought out methods, do provide against a lean purse in their mature years. For a lean purse to a man no longer able to earn, or to a family without its head is a sore tragedy.

"This then is the Sixth Remedy for a Lean Purse. Provide in advance for the needs of thy growing age and the protection of thy family."

NOTES: _____

_____

_____

_____

_____

_____

_____

_____

_____

_____

_____

_____

_____

_____

_____

_____

_____

_____

_____

THE SEVENTH REMEDY

Increase thy Ability to Earn

"This day do I speak to thee, my students, of one of the most vital remedies for a lean purse. Yet, I will talk not of gold, but of yourselves, of the men beneath the robes of many colors who do sit before me. I will talk to you of those things within the minds and lives of men, which do work for or against their success." So did Arkad address his class upon the seventh day.

"Not long ago, came to me a young man seeking to borrow. When I questioned him the cause of his necessity, he complained that his earnings were insufficient to pay his expenses. Thereupon, I explained to him, this being the case, he was a poor customer for the money lender, as he possessed no surplus earning capacity to repay the loan.

" 'What you need, young man', I told him, is to earn more coins. What dost thou to increase thy capacity to earn?'

" 'All that I can do', he replied. 'Six times within two moons have I approached my master to request my pay be increased, but without success. No man can go oftener than that.'

"We may smile at his simplicity, yet he did possess one of the vital requirements to increase his earnings. Within him was a strong desire to earn more, a proper and commendable desire.

"Preceding accomplishment must be desire. Thy desires must be strong and definite. General desires are but weak longings. For a man to wish to be rich is of little purpose. For a man to desire five pieces of gold is a tangible desire, which he can press to fulfillment. After he has backed his desire for five pieces of gold with strength of purpose to secure it, next he can find similar ways to obtain ten pieces, and then twenty pieces, and later a thousand pieces, and behold, he has become wealthy. In learning to secure his one definite small desire, he hath trained himself to secure a larger one. This is the process by which wealth is accumulated; first in small sums, then in larger ones, as a man learns and becomes more capable.

"Desires must be simple and definite. They defeat their own purpose should they be too many, too confusing, or beyond the training to accomplish.

"As a man perfecteth himself in his calling, even so doth his ability to earn increase. In those days when I was a humble scribe carving upon the clay for a few coppers each day, I observed that other workers did more than I, and were paid more. Therefore, did I determine that I would be exceeded by none. Nor did it take long for me to discover the reason for their greater success. More interest in my work, more concentration upon my task, more persistence in my effort, and behold, few men could carve more tablets in a day than I. With reasonable promptness, my increased skill was rewarded, nor was it necessary for me to go six times to my master to request recognition.

"The more of wisdom we know, the more we may earn. That man who seeks to learn more of his craft shall be richly rewarded. If he is an artisan, he may seek to learn the methods and the tools of those most skillful in the same line. If he laboreth at the law or at healing, he may consult and exchange knowledge with others of his calling. If he be a merchant, he may continually seek better goods that can be purchased at lower prices.

"Always do the affairs of man change and improve, because keen-minded men seek greater skill that they may better serve those upon whose patronage they depend. Therefore, I urge all men to be in the front rank of progress, and not to stand still, lest they be left behind.

"Many things come to make a man's life rich with gainful experiences. Such things as the following, a man must do if he shall respect himself: "He must pay his debts with all promptness, within his power, not purchasing that for which he is unable to pay.

"He must take care of his family, that they may think and speak well of him.

"He must make a will of record, that in case the Gods call him, proper and honorable division of his property be accomplished.

"He must have compassion upon those who are injured or smitten by misfortune, and aid them within reasonable limits. He must do deeds of thoughtfulness to those dear to him.

"Thus the seventh and last remedy for a lean purse is to cultivate thy own powers, to study and become wiser, to become more skillful, to so act as to respect thyself. Thereby shalt thou acquire confidence in thyself to achieve thy carefully considered desires.

"These then are the Seven Remedies for a Lean Purse, which, out of the experience of a long and successful life I do urge for all men who desire wealth.

"There is **MORE GOLD in BABYLON**, my students, than thou dreamest of. There is abundance for all!

"Go thou forth and practice these truths that thou mayest prosper and grow wealthy, as is thy right.

"Go thou forth and teach these truths that every honorable subject of his majesty may also share liberally in the ample wealth of our beloved city. **THIS IS THY KING'S COMMAND!**"

THE TALE OF THE GODDESS OF GOOD LUCK

This day I am lucky for I have found a
purse in which are pieces of gold. To
continue to be lucky is my great desire.

Chapter IV

THE TALE OF THE GODDESS OF GOOD LUCK

The Temple of Learning in old Babylon was an unusual institution. In this spacious building, many groups of men would congregate each evening about their favorite leaders to discuss interesting subjects.

Listen to Audio

Within the doors of this temple, all men met as equals. Here, the humblest slave could discuss upon an equal footing with a prince of the royal house.

Einstein
Thinkers
.com

https://MoreHelp.us/C-4 →

When Arkad arrived at his special corner upon a certain evening, four score men reclining upon the small rugs were awaiting him.

"What shall we discuss this night?" inquired Arkad.

"I have a subject," ventured a tall cloth weaver, arising as was the custom. 'This day I am lucky, for I have found a purse in which are pieces of gold. To continue to be lucky is my great desire. Feeling that all men share with me this desire, I do suggest we debate good luck. Let us seek to discover if there be ways it can be enticed to one."

"A most interesting subject has been offered to us," Arkad resumed. "To some, good luck bespeaks but a chance happening that may come to any man. Others do believe that the instigator of all good fortune is our most bounteous goddess, Ashtar, ever anxious to favor with generous gifts those who please her. What say you, my friends, shall we seek to find if there be means by which good luck may be enticed to visit each and all of us?"

"Yea! Yea! And much of it!" responded his listeners.

"To seek good luck requireth action upon our part. Who among you will offer a suggestion as to where we shall begin our search?" queried Arkad.

"'That I will do," spoke a well-robed youth, arising. "When a man speaketh of luck, is it not natural that his thoughts should turn to the gaming tables? Is it not there, where we may find many men courting the goddess, in the hope that she will favor them with rich winnings?"

"Continue thy story," called a voice as he resumed his seat. "Didst thou find the favor of the goddess there?"

"I am not averse to admitting, she seemed not to know that I was there," he replied. "How about you? Have you found her awaiting you in such places?"

"A wise start," broke in Arkad. "We meet here to consider all sides of each question. To ignore the gaming tables would be to pass by an instinct, quite common in most men, the love of taking a chance with the hope of winning."

"That doth remind me of the races yesterday," called another man. "If the goddess frequents the gaming tables, certainly she does not overlook the races which, to me, are far more pleasure. Tell us, Arkad, didst she whispers to you to bet upon those greys from Nineveh? I did stand right behind when thou placeth thy bet, and could scarce believe my ears, good as they are. You know as well as all of us that no team can beat our beloved bays. Does it not look as though the goddess whispered in his ear, that the inside black was to stumble as they made the last turn, and trip the bays to give the greys an unearned victory?"

Arkad smiled good humoredly at the banter. "What reason have we to think the good goddess would take that much interest in any man's bet upon a horse race? I feel that she is a goddess of love and dignity, whose pleasure it is to aid those who are in need, and to reward those who are deserving. I look to find her not at the gaming tables, where men lose more gold than they can win.

"In honest trading as in buying and selling, a man may expect to make a profit upon his transactions. Perhaps not upon all, because sometimes he may act without good judgment. But if he persists, he may usually expect to make his profit. This is so, because the chance of profit is always in his favor.

"But when a man playeth the games, the chance of profit is always against him, and always in favor of the game keeper. The game is so arranged to favor the keeper. It is his business at which he plans to make a liberal profit for himself. Few men realize how certain the game keeper's profit, and how poor their own chance to win.

"Thus, for an example, it will be well for us to consider wagering upon the cube. Each time it is cast, we bet which side will be uppermost. If it be the red side, the game master pays to us four times our bet. If it shows any one of the other five sides uppermost, we lose. Thus, the figures show that for each cast the player has five chances to lose, and because the red pays four to one, he has four chances to win. In a night's play, the game master expects to keep for his own one-fifth of all the wagers made. Can any man expect to win consistently against such odds so arranged that he should lose consistently?"

"Yet, some men do win large sums at times," volunteered one of the listeners.

"Quite so, they do," Arkad continued. "Realizing this, the thought has often come to me, whether money secured in such ways brings any worthwhile value to those who receive it. Among my acquaintances are many of the successful men of Babylon, yet among them I cannot name one who can trace his start to such a source. You, who are here tonight, must know a great many more of the substantial citizens of our city. To me, it would be of interest to learn how many of our better citizens can credit the gaming tables with their start or their support. What say you?"

There was a prolonged pause. Finally, a voice enquired, "Wouldst thy inquiry include the game keeper?"

"If not one of you can think of anyone else. But wait, how about yourselves? Are there any consistent winners with us here, who hesitate to advise us about the sources of their incomes?"

His challenge was answered by a loud groan from the rear, taken up and spread by others amid much laughter. "It would look that we were seeking far from where we should.

"Who among you has, at any time, had good luck such as our friend, the cloth weaver, finding gold or valuables? What, no one? Then, rare indeed be this kind of good luck. Who among you have had good luck within thy reach, only to let it escape?"

Many hands were raised.

"Speak up one of you! Let us hear how it could escape you. Who shall be the first?"

An elderly merchant arose, smoothing his genteel white robes. "With thy permission, most honorable Arkad, and friends, I will gladly relate a tale that doth illustrate how closely unto a man good luck may approach, and how blindly he may permit it to escape, much to his loss.

"Many years ago when a young man, just married and well started to earning, my father did come one day and urge most strongly that I enter upon an investment. The son of one of his good friends had taken notice of a barren tract of land not far beyond the outer walls of our city. It lay high above the canal where no water could reach it.

"The son of my father's friend devised a plan to purchase this land, build three large water wheels that could be operated by oxen, and thereby raise the life-giving waters to the fertile soil. This accomplished, he planned to divide into small tracts, and sell to the residents of the city for herb patches.

"The son of my father's friend did not possess sufficient gold to complete such an undertaking. Like myself, he was a young man earning a fair sum. His father, like mine, was a man of large family and small means. He, therefore, decided to interest a group of men to enter the enterprise with him. The group was to comprise twelve, each of whom must be a money earner and agree to pay one-tenth of his earnings into the enterprise until the land was made ready for sale. All would then share justly in the profits in proportion to their investment.

" 'Thou, my son', bespoke my father unto me, 'art now in thy young manhood. It is my deep desire that thou begin the building of a valuable estate for thyself that thou mayest become respected among men. I desire to see thou profit from a knowledge of the thoughtless mistakes of thy father'.

" 'This do I most ardently desire, my father," I replied.

" 'Then, this do I advise. Do what I should have done at thy age.

From thy earnings, keep out one-tenth to put into favorable investments. With this one-tenth of thy earnings, and what it will also earn, thou canst, before thou art my age, accumulate for thyself a valuable estate'.

" 'Thy words are words of wisdom, my father. Greatly do I desire riches. Yet there are many uses to which my earnings are called. Therefore, do I hesitate to do as thou dost advise. I am young. There is plenty of time'.

" 'So, I thought at thy age, yet behold, many years have passed, and I have not yet made the beginning'.

" 'We live in a different age, my father, I shall avoid thy mistakes'.

" 'Opportunity stands before thee, my son. It is offering a chance that may lead to wealth. I beg of thee, do not delay. Go upon the morrow to the son of my friend and bargain with him to pay ten percent of thy earnings into this investment. Go promptly upon the morrow. Opportunity waits for no man. Today it is here; soon it is gone. Therefore, delay not!'

"In spite of the advice of my father, I did hesitate. There were beautiful new robes just brought by the tradesmen from the East, robes of such richness and beauty, my good wife and I felt we must each possess one. Should I agree to pay one-tenth of my earnings into the enterprise, we must deprive ourselves of these and other pleasures we dearly desired. I delayed making a decision until it was too late, much to my subsequent regret. The enterprise did prove to be more profitable than any man had prophesied. This is my tale, showing how I did permit good luck to escape."

"In this tale, we see how good luck waits to come to that man who accepts opportunity," commented a swarthy man of the desert. "To the building of an estate, there must always be the beginning. That start may be a few pieces of gold or silver, which a man diverts from his earnings to his first investment. I, myself, am the owner of many herds. The start of my herds, I did begin when I was a mere boy, and did purchase with one piece of silver a young calf. This, being the beginning of my wealth, was of great importance to me.

"To take his first start to building an estate is as good luck as can come to any man. With all men, that first step, which changes them from men who earn from their own labor, to men who draw dividends from the earnings of their gold, is important. Some, fortunately, take it when young, and thereby outstrip in financial success those who do take it later, or those unfortunate men like the father of this merchant who never take it.

"Had our friend, the merchant, taken this step in his early manhood, when this opportunity came to him, this day, he would be blessed with much more of this world's goods. Should the good luck of our friend, the cloth weaver, cause him to take such a step at this time, it will indeed be but the beginning of much greater good fortune."

"Thank you! I like to speak, also." A stranger from another country arose. "I am a Syrian. Not so well do I speak your tongue. I wish to call this friend, the merchant, a name. Maybe you think it not polite, this name. Yet, I wish to call him that. But, alas, I not know your word for it. If I do call it in Syrian, you will not understand. Therefore, please some good gentlemen, tell me that right name you call man who puts off doing those things that mighty good for him."

"Procrastinator," called a voice.

"That's him," shouted the Syrian, waving his hands excitedly, "he accepts not opportunity when she comes. He waits. He says I have much business right now. Bye and bye I talk to you. Opportunity, she will not wait for such slow fellow. She thinks if a man desires to be lucky, he will step quick. Any man who not step quick when opportunity comes, he big procrastinator like our friend, this merchant."

The merchant arose and bowed good naturedly in response to the laughter. "My admiration to thee, stranger within our gates, who hesitates not to speak the truth."

"And now let us hear another tale of opportunity. Who has for us another experience?" demanded Arkad.

"I have," responded a red-robed man of middle age. "I am a buyer of animals, mostly camels and horses. Sometimes, I do also buy the sheep and goats. The tale I am about to relate will tell truthfully how opportunity came one night when I did least expect it. Perhaps, for this reason, I did let it escape. Of this, you shall be the judge.

"Returning to the city one evening, after a disheartening ten-day's journey in search of camels, I was much angered to find the gates of the city closed and locked. While my slaves spread our tent for the night, which we must spend with little food and no water, I was approached by an elderly farmer who, like ourselves, found himself locked outside.

" 'Honored sir', he addressed me, 'from thy appearance I do judge thee to be a buyer. If this be so, much would I like to sell to thee the most excellent flock of sheep just driven up. Alas, my good wife lies very sick with the fever. I must return with all haste. Buy thou my sheep, that I and my slaves may mount our camels and travel back without delay'.

"So dark it was that I could not see his flock, but from the bleating, I did know it must be large. Having wasted ten days searching for camels I could not find, I was glad to bargain with him. In his anxiety, he did set a most reasonable price. I accepted, well knowing my slaves could drive the flock through the city gates in the

62

morning, and sell at a substantial profit.

"The bargain concluded, I called my slaves to bring torches that we might count the flock, which the farmer declared to contain nine hundred. I shall not burden you, my friends, with a description of our difficulty in attempting to count so many thirsty, restless, milling sheep. It proved to be an impossible task. Therefore, I bluntly informed the farmer I would count them at daylight and pay him then.

" 'Please, most honorable sir,' he pleaded. 'Pay me but two-thirds of the price tonight that I may be on my way. I will leave my most intelligent and educated slave to assist to make the count in the morning. He is trustworthy, and to him thou canst pay the balance'.

"But I was stubborn, and refused to make payment that night. Next morning, before I awoke, the city gates opened and four buyers rushed out in search of flocks. They were most eager and willing to pay high prices, because the city was threatened with siege, and food was not plentiful. Nearly three times the price at which he had offered the flock to me, did the old farmer receive for it. Thus, was rare good luck allowed to escape."

"Here is a tale most unusual," commented Arkad. "What wisdom doth it suggest?"

"The wisdom of making a payment immediately when we are convinced our bargain is wise," suggested a venerable saddle maker. "If the bargain be good, then dost thou need protection against thy own weaknesses, as much as against any other man. We mortals are changeable. Alas, I must say more apt to change our minds when right than wrong. Wrong, we are stubborn indeed. Right, we are prone to vacillate and let opportunity escape. My first judgment is my best. Yet always, have I found it difficult to compel myself to proceed with a good bargain when made. Therefore, as a protection against my own weaknesses, I do make a prompt deposit thereon.

This doth save me from later regrets, for the good luck that should have been mine."

"Thank you! Again, I like to speak." The Syrian was upon his feet once more. "These tales much alike. Each time, opportunity flies away for same reason. Each time, she come to procrastinator, bringing good plan. Each time, they hesitate, not say, right now best time, I do it quick. How can men succeed that way?"

"Wise are thy words, my friend," responded the buyer. "Good luck fled from procrastination in both these tales. Yet, this is not unusual. The spirit of procrastination is within all men. We desire riches; yet, how often when opportunity doth appear before us, that spirit of procrastination from within doth urge various delays in our acceptance. In listening to it, we do become our own worst enemies.

"In my younger days, I did not know it by this long word our friend from Syria doth enjoy. I did think at first, it was my own poor judgment that did cause me loss of many profitable trades. Later, I did credit it to my stubborn disposition. At last, I did recognize it for what it was—a habit of needless delaying where action was required, action prompt and decisive. How I did hate it when its true character stood revealed. With the bitterness of a wild ass hitched to a chariot, I did break loose from this enemy to my success."

'Thank you! I like ask question from Mr. Merchant." The Syrian was speaking. "You wear fine robes, not like those of poor man. You speak like successful man. Tell us, do you listen now when procrastination whispers in your ear?"

"Like our friend the buyer, I also had to recognize and conquer procrastination," responded the merchant. "To me, it proved to be an enemy, ever watching and waiting to thwart my accomplishments. The tale I did relate, is but one of many similar instances I could tell, to show how it drove away my opportunities.

Tis not difficult to conquer, once understood. No man willingly permits the thief to rob his bins of grain. Nor does any man willingly permit an enemy to drive away his customers and rob him of his profits. When once I did recognize that such acts as these my enemy was committing, with determination, I conquered it. So, must every man master his own spirit of procrastination before he can expect to share in the rich treasures of Babylon.

"What sayest, Arkad? Because thou art the richest man in Babylon, many do proclaim thee to be the luckiest. Dost agree with me, that no man can arrive at a full measure of success, until he hath completely crushed the spirit of procrastination within him?"

"It is even as thou sayest," Arkad admitted. "During my long life, I have watched generation following generation, marching forward along those avenues of trade, science, and learning that lead to success in life. Opportunities came to all these men. Some grasped theirs and moved steadily to the gratification of their deepest desires, but the majority hesitated, faltered, and fell behind."

Arkad turned to the cloth weaver. "Thou didst suggest that we debate good luck. Let us hear what thou now thinkest upon the subject."

"I do see good luck in a different light. I had thought of it as something most desirable, that might happen to a man without effort upon his part. Now, I do realize such happenings are not the sort of thing one may attract to himself. From our discussion, have I learned that to attract good luck to oneself, it is necessary to take advantage of opportunities. Therefore, in the future, I shall endeavor to make the best of such opportunities as do come to me."

"Thou hast well grasped the truths brought forth in our discussion," Arkad replied. "Good luck, we do find, often follows opportunity, but seldom comes otherwise. Our merchant friend would have found great good luck, had he accepted the opportunity the good goddess did present to him. Our friend the buyer, likewise, would have enjoyed good luck, had he completed the purchase of the flock, and sold at such a handsome profit.

"We did pursue this discussion to find a means by which good luck could be enticed to us. I feel that we have found the way. Both the tales did illustrate how good luck follows opportunity. Herein lies a truth, that many similar tales of good luck, won or lost, could not change. The truth is this: good luck can be enticed by accepting opportunities.

'Those eager to grasp opportunities for their betterment, do attract the interest of the good goddess. She is ever anxious to aid those who please her. Men of action please her best. Therefore, if a plan be for thy best interest, promptly accept it. If it be against thy best interest, with equal promptness, reject it.

"ACTION will lead thee forward to the successes thou dost desire.

Actions are favored by The Goddess of Good Luck

THE TALE OF THE FIVE LAWS OF GOLD

*With wisdom, gold can be secured
by those who have it not, as these
three bags of gold do prove.*

Chapter V

The Tale of The Five Laws of Gold

A bag heavy with gold or a clay tablet carved with words of wisdom; if thou hadst thy choice, which wouldst thou choose?"

By the flickering light from the fire of desert shrubs, the sun-tanned faces of his listeners gleamed with interest.

Listen to Audio

"The GOLD, the GOLD," chorused the twenty-seven.

https://MoreHelp.us/C-5 →

Old Kalabab smiled knowingly.

"Hark," he resumed, raising his hand. "Hear the wild dogs out there in the night. They howl and wail because they are lean with hunger. Yet feed them, and what do they? Fight and strut. Then fight and strut some more, giving no thought to the morrow that will surely come.

"Just so it is with the sons of men. Give them a choice of gold and wisdom—what do they do? Ignore the wisdom and waste the gold. On the morrow they wail because they have no more gold.

"Gold is reserved for those who know its laws and abide by them."

Kalabab drew his white robe close about his lean legs, for a cool night wind was blowing. "Because thou hast served me faithfully upon our long journey, because thou cared well for my camels, because thou toiled uncomplainingly across the hot sands of the desert, because thou fought bravely the robbers that sought to despoil my merchandise, I will tell thee this night the tale of, 'THE

FIVE LAWS OF GOLD', such a tale as thou never hast heard before."

"Hark ye, with deep attention to the words I speak, for if you grasp their meaning and heed them, in the days that come, thou shalt have much gold."

He paused impressively. Above in a canopy of blue, the stars shone brightly in the crystal-clear skies of Babylonia. Behind the group, loomed their faded tents tightly staked against possible desert storms. Beside the tents were neatly stacked bales of merchandise covered with skins. Nearby, the camel herd sprawled in the sand, some chewing their cuds contentedly, others snoring in hoarse discord.

"Thou hast told us many good tales, Kalabab," spoke up the chief packer. "We look to thy wisdom to guide us upon the morrow, when our service with thee shall be at an end."

"I have but told thee of my adventures in strange and distant lands, but this night, I shall tell thee of the wisdom of Arkad, the wise rich man."

"The gold, the gold!" chorused the twenty-seven.

"Much have we heard of him," acknowledged the chief packer, "for he was the richest man that ever lived in Babylon."

"The richest man he was, and that because he was wise in the ways of gold, even as no man had ever been before him. This night shall I tell of his great wisdom, as it was told to me by Nomasir, his son, many years ago in Nineveh, when I was but a lad.

"My master and myself had tarried long into the night in the palace of Nomasir. I had helped my master bring great bundles of fine rugs, each one to be tried by Nomasir until his choice of colors was satisfied. At last, he was well pleased and commanded us to sit with him and to drink a rare vintage, odorous to the nostrils and most warming to my stomach, which was unaccustomed to such a drink. "Then, did he tell us this tale of the great wisdom of Arkad, his father, even as I shall tell it to you.

"In Babylon, it is the custom, as you know, that the sons of wealthy fathers live with their parents in expectation of inheriting the estate. Arkad did not approve of this custom. Therefore, when Nomasir reached man's estate, he sent for the young man and addressed him: " 'My son, it is my desire that thou succeed to my estate. Thou must, however, first prove that thou art capable of wisely handling it. Therefore, I wish that thou go out into the world, and show thy ability both to acquire gold, and to make thyself respected among men.

" 'To start thee well, I will give thee two things of which I, myself, was denied when I started as a poor youth to build up a fortune.

" 'First, I give thee this bag of gold. If thou use it wisely, it will be the basis of thy future success.

" 'Second, I give thee this clay tablet upon which is carved "THE

FIVE LAWS OF GOLD." If thou dost but interpret them in thy own acts, they shall bring thee competence and security.

" Ten years from this day come thou back to the house of thy father and give account of thyself. If thou prove worthy, I will then make thee the heir to my estate. Otherwise, I will give it to the priests, that they barter for my soul the kind consideration of the gods.'

"So Nomasir went forth to make his own way, taking his bag of gold, the clay tablet carefully wrapped in silken cloth, his slave, and the horses upon which they rode.

"The ten years passed, and Nomasir, as he had agreed, returned to the house of his father, who provided a great feast in his honor, to which he invited many friends and relatives. After the feast was over, the father and mother mounted their thronelike seats at one side of the great hall, and Nomasir stood before them to give an account of himself, as he had promised his father.

"It was evening. The room was hazy with smoke from the wicks of the oil lamps that but dimly lighted it. Slaves in white woven jackets and tunics fanned the humid air rhythmically with long-stemmed palm leaves. A stately dignity colored the scene. The wife of Nomasir and his two young sons, with friends and other members of the family, sat upon rugs behind him, eager listeners.

" 'My father,' he began deferentially, 'I bow before thy wisdom. Ten years ago, when I stood at the gates of manhood, thou bade me go forth and become a man among men, instead of remaining a vassal to thy fortune.

" 'Thou gave me liberally of thy gold. Thou gave me liberally of thy wisdom. Of the gold, alas! I must admit of a disastrous handling. It fled, indeed, from my inexperienced hands, even as a wild hare flees at the first opportunity from the youth who captures it.'

"The father smiled indulgently. 'Continue, my son, thy tale interests me in all its details.'

" 'I decided to go to Nineveh, as it was a growing city, believing that I might find there opportunities. I joined a caravan, and among its members made numerous friends. Two well-spoken men, who had a most beautiful white horse as fleet as the wind, were among these.

" 'As we journeyed, they told me in confidence that in Nineveh was a wealthy man who owned a horse so swift that it had never been beaten. Its owner believed that no horse living could run with greater speed. Therefore, would he wager any sum, however large, that his horse could out-speed any horse in all Babylonia. Compared to their horse, so my friends said, it was but a lumbering ass that could be beaten with ease.

" 'They offered, as a great favor, to permit me to join them in a wager. I was quite carried away with the plan.

" 'Our horse was badly beaten, and I lost much of my gold.' The father laughed. 'Later, I discovered that this was a deceitful plan of these men, and they constantly journeyed with caravans seeking victims. You see, the man in Nineveh was their partner, and shared with them the bets he won. This shrewd deceit taught me my first lesson in looking out for myself.

" 'I was soon to learn another, equally bitter. In the caravan was another young man with whom I became quite friendly. He was the son of wealthy parents and like myself, journeying to Nineveh to find a suitable location. Not long after our arrival, he told me that a merchant had died, and his shop with its rich merchandise and patronage could be secured at a paltry price. Saying that we would be equal partners, but first, he must return to Babylon to secure his gold, he prevailed upon me to purchase the stock with my gold, agreeing that his would be used later to carry on our venture.

At this time I bethought me of the tablet upon
which thou had carved, The Five Laws of Gold.

" 'He long delayed the trip to Babylon, proving in the meantime to be an unwise buyer and a foolish spender. I finally put him out, but not before the business had deteriorated to where we had only unsaleable goods and no gold to buy other goods. I sacrificed what was left to an Israelite for a pitiful sum.

" 'Soon there followed, I tell you, my father, bitter days. I sought employment and found it not, for I was without trade or training that would enable me to earn. I sold my horses. I sold my slave. I sold my extra robes that I might have food and a place to sleep, but each day grim want crouched closer.

" 'But in those bitter days, I remembered thy confidence in me, my father. Thou hadst sent me forth to become a man, and this I was determined to accomplish.' The mother buried her face and wept softly.

" 'At this time, I bethought me of the tablet thou had given to me upon which thou had carved, "THE FIVE LAWS OF GOLD." Thereupon, I read most carefully thy words of wisdom, and realized that had I but sought wisdom first, my gold would not have been lost to me. I learned by heart each law, determined that when once more the goddess of good fortune smiled upon me, I would be guided by the wisdom of age and not by the inexperience of youth.

" 'For the benefit of you who are seated here this night, I will read the wisdom of my father as engraved upon the clay tablet which he gave to me ten years ago.'

NOTES: _____

_____

_____

_____

_____

_____

_____

_____

_____

_____

_____

_____

_____

_____

_____

_____

_____

_____

_____

_____

_____

THE FIVE LAWS OF GOLD

I. Gold cometh gladly and in increasing quantity to any man whosoever will put by not less than one tenth of his earnings to create an estate for his future and that of his family.

II. Gold laboreth diligently and contentedly for the wise owner who finds for it profitable employment, multiplying even as the flocks of the field.

III. Gold clingeth to the protection of the cautious owner who invests it under the advice of men wise in its handling.

IV. Gold slippeth away from the man who invests it in businesses or purposes with which he is not familiar or which are not approved by those skilled in its keep.

V. Gold flees the man who would force it to impossible earnings or who followeth the alluring advice of tricksters and schemers or who trusts it to his own inexperience and romantic desires in investment.

" 'These are the five laws of gold as written by my father. I do proclaim them as of greater value than gold itself, as I will show by the continuance of my tale.'

"He again faced his father. 'I have told thee of the depth of poverty and despair to which my inexperience brought me.

" 'However, there is no chain of disasters that will not come to an end. Mine came when I secured employment managing a crew of slaves working upon the new outer wall of the city.

" 'Profiting from my knowledge of the first law of gold, I saved a copper from my first earnings, adding to it at every opportunity until I had a piece of silver. It was a slow procedure, for one must live. I did spend grudgingly, I admit, because I was determined to earn back before the ten years were over, as much gold as you, my Father, had given to me.

" 'One day the slave master with whom I had become quite friendly, said to me: Thou art a thrifty youth who spends not wantonly what he earns. Hast thou gold put by that is not earning?"

" 'Yes,' I replied, 'it is my greatest desire to accumulate gold to replace that which my father gave to me and which I have lost.'

Tis a worthy ambition, I will grant, and do you know that the gold which you have saved can work for you and earn much more gold?'

" 'Alas! my experience has been bitter, for my father's gold has fled from me, and I am in much fear lest my own do the same.'

" 'If thou hast confidence in me, I will give thee a lesson in the profitable handling of gold,' he replied. 'Within a year, the outer wall will be complete, and ready for the great gates of bronze that will be built at each entrance, to protect the city from the king's enemies. In all Nineveh, there is not enough metal to make these gates, and the king has not thought to provide it. Here is my plan: A group of us will pool our gold, and send a caravan to the mines of copper and tin, which are distant, and bring to Nineveh the metal for the gates. When the king says, 'Make the great gates,' we alone can supply the metal, and a rich price he will pay. If the king will not buy from us, we will yet have the metal, which can be sold for a fair price.'

" 'In his offer, I recognized an opportunity to abide by the third law, and invest my savings under the guidance of wise men. Nor was I disappointed. Our pool was a success, and my small store of gold was greatly increased by the transaction.

" 'In due time, I was accepted as a member of this same group in other ventures. They were men wise in the profitable handling of gold. They talked over each plan presented with great care, before entering upon it. They would take no chance on losing their principal, or tying it up in unprofitable investments, from which their gold could not be recovered. Such foolish things, as the horse race and the partnership into which I had entered with my inexperience, would have had scant consideration with them. They would have immediately pointed out their weaknesses.

" 'Through my association with these men, I learned to safely invest gold to bring profitable returns. As the years went on, my treasure increased more and more rapidly. I not only made back as much as I lost, but much more.

" 'Through my misfortunes, my trials, and my success, I have tested time and again the wisdom of the Five Laws of Gold, my father, and have proven them true in every test. To him who is without knowledge of the Five Laws, Gold comes not often, and goeth away quickly. But to him who abideth by the Five Laws, Gold comes and works as his dutiful slave.'

"Nomasir ceased speaking and motioned to a slave in the back of the room. The slave brought forward, one at a time, three heavy leather bags. One of these Nomasir took and placed upon the floor before his father addressing him again:

" 'Thou did give to me a bag of gold, Babylon gold. Behold in its place, I do return to thee a bag of Nineveh gold of equal weight. An equal exchange as all will agree.

" 'Thou didst give to me a clay tablet inscribed with wisdom. Behold, in its stead, I do return two bags of gold.' So saying, he took from the slave the other two bags and, likewise, placed them upon the floor before his father.

In his offer, I recognized an opportunity to abide by the Third Law and invest my savings under the guidance of wise men.

" 'This I do to prove to thee, my father, of how much greater value I consider thy wisdom than thy gold. Yet, who can measure in bags of gold, the value of wisdom? Without wisdom, gold is quickly lost by those who have it, but with wisdom, gold can be secured by those who have it not, as these three bags of gold do prove.

" 'It does, indeed, give to me the deepest satisfaction, my father, to stand before thee and say that, because of thy wisdom, I have been able to become rich and respected before men.'

"The father placed his hand fondly upon the head of Nomasir. 'Thou hast learned well thy lessons, and I am, indeed, fortunate to have a son to whom I may entrust my wealth.' "

Kalabab ceased his tale, and looked critically at his listeners.

"What means this to thee, this tale of Nomasir?" he continued.

"Who amongst thee can go to thy father, or to the father of thy wife, and give an account of wise handling of his earnings?

"What would these venerable men think were you to say, 'I have traveled much and learned much and labored much and earned much, yet alas, of gold I have little. Some I spent wisely, some I spent foolishly, and much I lost in unwise ways.'

"Dost still think it but an inconsistency of fate that some men have much gold and others have naught? Then you err.

"Men have much gold when they know the Five Laws of Gold and abide thereby.

"Because I learned these Five Laws in my youth, and abided by them, I have become a wealthy merchant. Not by some strange magic did I accumulate my wealth.

"Wealth that comes quickly, goeth the same way.

"Wealth that stayeth to give enjoyment and satisfaction to its owner, comes gradually, because it is a child born of knowledge and persistent purpose.

'To earn wealth is but a slight burden upon the thoughtful man. Bearing the burden consistently from year to year accomplishes the final purpose.

"The Five Laws of Gold offer to thee a rich reward for their observance.

"Each of these Five Laws is rich with meaning, and lest thou overlook this in the briefness of my tale, I will now repeat them. I do know them each by heart, because in my youth, I could see their value and would not be content until I knew them word for word.

The First Law of Gold

> *Gold cometh gladly and in increasing quantity to any man whosoever will put by not less than one-tenth of his earnings to create an estate for his future and that of his family.*

"Any man who will put by one-tenth of his earnings consistently, and invest it wisely, will surely create a valuable estate that will provide an income for him in the future, and further guarantee safety for his family, in case the gods call him to the world of darkness. This law also sayeth that gold cometh gladly to such a man. I can truly certify this in my own life. The more gold I accumulate, the more readily it comes to me, and in increased quantities. The gold which I save earns more, even as yours will, and its earnings earn more, and this is the working out of the first law."

NOTES: _____

_____

_____

_____

_____

_____

_____

_____

_____

_____

The Second Law of Gold

> *Gold laboreth diligently and contentedly, for the wise owner who finds for it profitable employment, multiplying even as the flocks of the field.*

"Gold, indeed, is a willing worker. It is ever eager to multiply when the opportunity presents itself. To every man who hath a store of gold set by, opportunity comes for its most profitable use. As the years pass, it multiplies itself in surprising fashion."

NOTES: _____

_____

_____

_____

_____

_____

_____

_____

_____

_____

_____

_____

_____

_____

_____

The Third Law of Gold

> *Gold clingeth to the protection of the cautious owner who invests it under the advice of men wise in its handling.*

Gold, indeed, clingeth to the cautious owner, even as it flees the careless owner. The man who seeks the advice of men wise in handling gold, soon learneth not to jeopardize his treasure, but to preserve in safety and to enjoy in contentment its consistent increase."

They would take no chance of losing their principal or tying it up in unprofitable investments.

NOTES: _____

_____

_____

_____

_____

_____

The Fourth Law of Gold

> *Gold slippeth away from the man who invests it in businesses or purposes with which he is not familiar, or which are not approved by those skilled in its keep.*

"To the man who hath gold, yet is not skilled in its handling, many uses for it appear most profitable. Too often these are fraught with the danger of loss, and if properly analyzed by wise men, show small possibility of profit. Therefore, the inexperienced owner of gold who trusts to his own judgment and invests it in business or purposes with which he is not familiar, too often finds his judgment imperfect, and pays with his treasure for his inexperience. Wise, indeed, is he who investeth his treasures under the advice of men skilled in the ways of gold."

NOTES: _____

_____

_____

_____

_____

_____

_____

_____

_____

_____

The Fifth Law of Gold

> *Gold flees the man who would force it to impossible earnings, or who followeth the alluring advice of tricksters and schemers, or who trusts it to his own inexperience and romantic desires in its investment.*

Gold flees the man who would force it to impossible earnings, or who followeth the alluring advice of tricksters and schemers, or who trusts it to his own inexperience and romantic desires in its investment.

"Fanciful propositions that thrill like adventure tales always come to the new owner of gold. These appear to endow his treasure with magic powers, that will enable it to make impossible earnings. Yet heed ye the wise men, for verily they know the risks that lurk behind every plan to make great wealth suddenly.

"Forget not the rich men of Nineveh, who would take no chance of losing their principal or tying it up in unprofitable investments.

"This ends my tale of 'The Five Laws of Gold.' In telling it to thee, I have told the secrets of my own success.

"Yet, they are not secrets, but truths, which every man must first learn and then follow, who wishes to step out of the multitude that, like yon wild dogs, must worry each day for food to eat.

"Tomorrow, we enter Babylon. Look! See the fire that burns eternal above the Temple of Bel! We are already in sight of the golden city. Tomorrow, each of thee shall have gold, the gold thou hast so well earned by thy faithful services.

"Ten years from this night, what can you tell about this gold?

"If there be men among you, who, like Nomasir, will use a portion of their gold to start for themselves an estate, and be thenceforth wisely guided by the wisdom of Arkad, ten years from now, 'tis a safe wager, like the son of Arkad, they will be rich and respected among men.

"Our wise acts accompany us through life to please us and to help us. Just as surely, our unwise acts follow us to plague and torment us. Alas, they cannot be forgotten. In the front rank of the torments that do follow us, are the memories of the things we should have done, of the opportunities which came to us and we took not.

"Rich is the Treasures of Babylon, so rich no man can count their value in pieces of gold. Each year, they grow richer and more valuable. Like the treasures of every land, they are a reward, a rich reward awaiting those men of purpose who determine to secure their just share.

"In the strength of thine own desires is a magic power. Guide this power with thy knowledge of 'The Five Laws of Gold', and thou shalt share the Treasures of Babylon."

NOTES: _____

_____

_____

_____

_____

_____

_____

Chapter VI

The Tale of The Gold Lender of Babylon

*From each person to whom I lend
I do exact a token for my token chest.*

THE TALE OF THE GOLD LENDER OF BABYLON

FIFTY PIECES OF GOLD! Never before had Rodan, the spearmaker of old Babylon, carried so much gold in his leather wallet. Happily, down the king's highway, from the palace of his most liberal Majesty, he strode. Cheerfully the gold clinked as the wallet at his belt swayed with each step — the sweetest music he had ever heard.

Fifty pieces of gold! All his! He could hardly realize his good fortune. What power in those clinking discs! They could purchase anything he wanted, a grand house, land, cattle, camels, horses, chariots, whatever he might desire.

Listen to Audio

https://MoreHelp.us/C-6 →

What use should he make of it? This evening, as he turned into a side street towards the home of his sister, he could think of nothing he would rather possess than those same glittering, heavy pieces of gold—his to keep.

It was upon an evening, some days later, that a perplexed Rodan entered the shop of Mathon, the lender of gold, and dealer in jewels and rare fabrics. Glancing neither to the right nor the left at the colorful articles artfully displayed, he passed through to the living quarters at the rear. Here he found the genteel Mathon lounging upon a rug, partaking of a meal served by a black slave.

"I would counsel with thee, for I know not what to do." Rodan stood stolidly, feet apart, hairy breast exposed by the gaping front of his leather jacket.

Mathon's narrow, sallow face smiled a friendly greeting. "What indiscretions hast thou done that thou shouldst seek the lender of gold? Hast been unlucky at the gaming table? Or hath some plump dame entangled thee? For many years have I known thee, yet never before hast thou sought me to aid thee in thy troubles."

"No, no. Not such as that. I seek no gold. Instead, I crave thy wise advice."

"Hear! Hear! What this man doth say. No one comes to the lender of gold for advice. My ears must play me false."

"They listen true."

"Can this be so? Rodan, the spearmaker, doth display more cunning than all the rest, for he comes to Mathon, not for gold, but for advice. Many men come to me for gold to pay for their follies, but as for advice, they want it not. Yet, who is more able to advise than the lender of gold, to whom many men come in trouble?

"Thou shalt eat with me, Rodan," he continued. "Thou shalt be my guest for the evening. Ando!" he commanded of the black slave, "draw up a rug for my friend, Rodan the spearmaker, who comes for advice. He shall be my honored guest. Bring to him much food, and get for him my largest cup. Choose well of the best wine, that he may have satisfaction in the drinking.

"Tell me what troubles thee."

"It is the king's gift."

"The king's gift? The king did make thee a gift, and it gives thee trouble? What manner of gift?"

"Because he was much pleased with the design I did submit to him for a new point on the spears of the royal guard, he did present me with fifty pieces of gold, and now I am much perplexed.

"I am beseeched each hour the sun doth travel across the sky by those who would share it with me."

"That is natural. More men want gold than have it, and would wish one who comes by it easily to divide. But can you not say 'No'? Is thy will not as strong as thy fist?"

"To many I can say no, yet sometimes it would be easier to say yes. Can one refuse to share with one's only sister, to whom he is deeply devoted?"

"Surely, thy own sister would not wish to deprive thee of enjoying thy reward."

"But it is for the sake of Araman, her husband, whom she wishes to see a rich merchant. She does feel that he has never had a chance, and she beseeches me to loan to him this gold, that he may become a prosperous merchant and repay me from his profits."

"My friend," resumed Mathon, " 'tis a worthy subject thou bringest to discuss. Gold bringeth unto its possessor responsibility, and a changed position with his fellow men. It bringeth fear, lest he lose it or it be tricked away from him. It bringeth a feeling of power and ability to do good. Likewise, it bringeth opportunities, whereby his very good intentions may bring him into difficulties.

"Didst ever hear of the farmer of Nineveh, who could understand the language of animals? I wot not, for 'tis not the kind of tale men like thee tell over the bronze caster's forge. I will tell it to thee, for thou shouldst know that to borrowing and lending there is more than the passing of gold from the hands of one to the hands of another.

"This farmer who could understand what the animals said to each other, did linger in the farm yard each evening just to listen to their words. One evening, he did hear the ox bemoaning to the ass the hardness of his lot. 'I do labor, pulling the plow from morning until night. No matter how hot the day, or how tired my legs, or how the bow doth chafe my neck, still must I work. But you are a creature of leisure. You are trapped with a colorful blanket, and do nothing more than carry our master about where he wishes to go. When he goes nowhere, you do rest and eat the green grass all the day.

"Now the ass, in spite of his vicious heels, was a goodly fellow and sympathized with the ox. 'My good friend', he replied, 'you do work very hard, and I would help ease your lot. Therefore, will I tell you how you may have a day of rest. In the morning, when the slave comes to fetch you to the plow, lie upon the ground and bellow much that he may say you are sick and cannot work.'

"So the ox took the advice of the ass, and the next morning the slave returned to the farmer, and told him the ox was sick, and could not pull the plow.

" 'Then', said the farmer, 'hitch the ass to the plow for the plowing must go on.'

Can one refuse to share with one's only sister?

"All that day the ass, who had only intended to help his friend, found himself compelled to do the ox's task. When night came, and he was released from the plow, his heart was bitter, and his legs were weary, and his neck was sore where the bow had chafed it. "The farmer lingered in the barnyard to listen. "The ox began first. 'You are my good friend. Because of your wise advice, I have enjoyed a day of rest'.

" 'And I', retorted the ass, 'am like many another simple hearted one, who starts to help a friend, and ends up by doing his task for him. Hereafter you draw your own plow, for I did hear the master tell the slave to send for the butcher were you sick again. I wish he would, for you are a lazy fellow'. Thereafter, they spoke to each other no more—this ended their friendship. Canst thou tell the moral to this tale, Rodan?"

" Tis a good tale," responded Rodan, "but I see not the moral."

"I thought not that you would. But it is there, and simple too. Just this: If thou desire to help thy friend, do so in a way that will not bring thy friend's burdens upon thyself."

"I had not thought of that. It is a wise moral. I wish not to assume the burdens of my sister's husband. But tell me. You lend to many. Do not the borrowers repay?"

Mathon smiled the smile of one whose soul is rich with much experience. "Could a loan be well made if the borrower cannot repay?

Must not the lender be wise and judge carefully whether his gold can perform a useful purpose to the borrower, and return to him once more; or whether it will be wasted by one unable to use it wisely, and leave him without his treasure, and leave the borrower with a debt he cannot repay? I will show to thee the tokens in my token chest, and let them tell thee some of their stories."

Into the room, he brought a chest as long as his arm, covered with red pigskin, and ornamented with bronze designs. He placed it upon the floor, and squatted before it, both hands upon the lid.

"From each person to whom I lend, I do exact a token for my token chest, to remain there until the loan is repaid. When they repay, I give back, but if they never repay, it will always remind me of one who was not faithful to my confidence.

"The safest loans, my token box tells me, are to those whose possessions are of more value than the loan they desire. They own lands, or jewels, or camels, or other things which could be sold to repay the loan. Some of the tokens given to me are jewels of more value than the loan. Others are promises that if the loan be not repaid as agreed, they will deliver to me certain property in settlement. On loans like those, I am assured that my gold will be returned with the rental thereon, for the loan is based on property.

"In another class are those who have the capacity to earn. They are such as you, who labor or serve and are paid. They have income, and if they are honest and suffer no misfortune, I know that they also can repay the gold I loan them and the rental to which I am entitled. Such loans are based on human effort.

"Others are those who have neither property nor assured earning capacity. Life is hard, and there will always be some who cannot adjust themselves to it. Alas, for the loans I make them, even though they be no larger than a pence, my token box may censure me in the years to come, unless they be guaranteed by good friends of the borrower who know him honorable."

Mathon released the clasp and opened the lid. Rodan leaned forward eagerly.

At the top of the chest, a bronze neck-piece lay upon a scarlet cloth. Mathon picked up the piece and patted it affectionately. "This shall always remain in my token chest, because the owner has passed on into the great darkness. I treasure it, his token, and I treasure his memory; for he was my good friend. We traded together with much success, until out of the east, he brought a woman to wed, beautiful, but not like our women. A dazzling creature. He spent his gold lavishly to gratify her desires. He came to me in distress when his gold was gone. I counselled with him. I told him I would help him to once more master his own affairs. He swore by the sign of the Great Bull that he would. But it was not to be. In a quarrel, she thrust a knife into the heart he dared her to pierce."

"And she?" questioned Rodan.

"Yes, of course, this was hers." He picked up the scarlet cloth. "In bitter remorse, she threw herself into the Euphrates. These two loans will never be repaid. The chest tells you, Rodan, that humans in the throes of great emotions are not safe risks for the gold lender.

He doth insist on repaying promptly.

"Here! Now this is different." He reached for a ring carved of ox bone. "This belongs to a farmer. I buy the rugs of his women. The locusts came, and they had not food. I helped him, and when the new crop came, he repaid me. Later, he came again and told of strange goats in a distant land as described by a traveler. They had long hair, so fine and soft it would weave into rugs more beautiful than any ever seen in Babylon. He wanted a herd, but he had no money. So, I did lend him gold to make the journey and bring back goats. Now his herd is begun, and next year I shall surprise the lords of Babylon with the most expensive rugs it has been their good fortune to buy. Soon I must return his ring. He doth insist on repaying promptly."

"Some borrowers do that?" queried Rodan.

"If they borrow for purposes that bring money back to them, I find it so. But if they borrow because of their indiscretions, I warn thee to be cautious if thou wouldst ever have thy gold back in hand again."

"Tell me about this," requested Rodan, picking up a heavy gold bracelet inset with jewels in rare designs.

"The women do appeal to my good friend," bantered Mathon.

"I am still much younger than you," retorted Rodan.

"I grant that, but this time thou doth suspicion romance where it is not. The owner of this is fat and wrinkled, and doth talk so much, and say so little she drives me mad. Once they had much money and were my good customers, but ill times came upon them. She has a son, of whom she would make a merchant. So, she came to me and borrowed gold, that he might become a partner of a caravan owner who travels with his camels, bartering in one city, what he buys in another.

"This man proved a rascal, for he left the poor boy in a distant city without money and without friends, pulling out early while the youth slept. Perhaps when this youth has grown to manhood, he will repay; until then, I get no rental for the loan—only much talk. But I do admit, the jewels are worthy of the loan."

"Did this lady ask thy advice as to the wisdom of the loan?"

"Quite otherwise. She had pictured to herself this son of hers, as a wealthy and powerful man of Babylon. To suggest the contrary was to infuriate her. A fair rebuke I had. I knew the risk for this inexperienced boy, but as she offered security, I could not refuse her.

"This," continued Mathon, waving a bit of pack rope tied into a knot, "belongs to Nebatur, the camel trader. When he would buy a herd larger than his funds, he brings to me this knot, and I lend to him according to his needs. He is a wise trader. I have confidence in his good judgment, and can lend him freely. Many other merchants of Babylon have my confidence because of their honorable behavior. Their tokens come and go frequently in my token box. Good merchants are an asset to our city, and it profits me to aid them to keep trade moving, that Babylon be prosperous."

Mathon picked out a beetle carved in turquoise and tossed it contemptuously on the floor. "A bug from Egypt. The lad who owns this does not care whether I ever receive back my gold. When I reproach him, he replies, 'How can I repay when ill fate pursues me? You have plenty more'. What can I do, the token is his father's—a worthy man of small means who did pledge his land and herd to back his son's enterprises? The youth found success at first, and then was over-zealous to gain great wealth. His knowledge was immature. His enterprises collapsed.

"Youth is ambitious. Youth would take short cuts to wealth and the desirable things for which it stands. To secure wealth quickly, youth often borrows unwisely. Youth, never having had experience, cannot realize that hopeless debt is like a deep pit into which one may descend quickly, and where one may struggle vainly for many days. It is a pit of sorrow and regrets, where the brightness of the sun is overcast, and night is made unhappy by restless sleeping. Yet, I do not discourage borrowing gold. I encourage it. I recommend it, if it be for a wise purpose. I myself made my first real success as a merchant with borrowed gold.

"Yet, what should the lender do in such a case? The youth is in despair and accomplishes nothing. He is discouraged. He makes no effort to repay. My heart turns against depriving the father of his land and cattle."

"You tell me much that I am interested to hear," ventured Rodan, "but, I hear no answer to my question. Should I lend my fifty pieces of gold to my sister's husband? They mean much to me."

Pulling out early while the youth still sleep.

"Thy sister is a sterling woman, whom I do much esteem. Should her husband come to me and ask to borrow fifty pieces of gold, I should ask him for what purpose he would use it.

"If he answered that he desired to become a merchant like myself, and deal in jewels and rich furnishings, I would say, 'What knowledge have you of the ways of trade? Do you know where you can buy at lowest cost? Do you know where you can sell at a fair price?' Could he say 'Yes' to these questions?"

"No, he could not," Rodan admitted. "He has helped me much in making spears, and he has helped some in the shops."

"Then, would I say to him that his purpose was not wise. Merchants must learn their trade. His ambition, though worthy, is not practical, and I would not lend him any gold.

"But, supposing he could say, 'Yes, I have helped merchants much. I know how to travel to Smyrna and to buy at low cost the rugs the housewives weave. I also know many of the rich people of Babylon to whom I can sell these at a large profit.' Then I would say: 'Your purpose is wise and your ambition honorable. I shall be glad to lend you the fifty pieces of gold, if you can give me security that they will be returned.' But would he say, 'I have no security other than that I am an honored man and will pay you well for the loan.' Then would I reply, 'I treasure much each piece of gold. Were the robbers to take it from you as you journeyed to Smyrna, or take the rugs from you as you returned, then you would have no means of repaying me and my gold would be gone.'

"Gold, you see, Rodan, is the merchandise of the lender of money. It is easy to lend. If it is lent unwisely, then it is difficult to get back. The wise lender wishes not the risk of the undertaking, but the guarantee of safe repayment.

" 'Tis well," he continued, "to assist those that are in trouble, 'tis well to help those upon whom fate has laid a heavy hand. 'Tis well to help those who are starting, that they may progress and become valuable citizens. But help must be given wisely, lest, like the farmer's ass, in our desire to help, we but take upon ourselves the burden that belongs to another.

"Again I wandered from thy question, Rodan, but hear my answer: Keep thy fifty pieces of gold. What thy labor earns for thee and what is given thee for reward is thine own, and no man can put an obligation upon thee to part with it, unless it be thy wish. If wouldst lend it so that it may earn thee more gold, then lend with caution, and in many places. I like not idle gold, even less, I like too much of risk.

"How many years hast thou labored as a spear-maker?"

"Fully three."

"How much besides the King's gift hast saved?"

"Three gold pieces."

"Each year that thou hast labored, thou hast denied thyself good things to save from thine earnings one piece of gold?"

" 'Tis as you say."

"Then mightest save in fifty years of labor fifty pieces of gold by thy self-denial?"

"A lifetime of labor it would be."

"Thinkest thou thy sister would wish to jeopardize the savings of fifty years of labor over the bronze melting pot that her husband might experiment on being a merchant?"

"Not if I spoke in your words."

"Then go to her and say, 'Three years I have labored each day except fast days, from morning until night, and I have denied myself many things that my heart craved. For each year of labor and self-denial, I have to show one piece of gold. Thou art my favored sister, and I wish that thy husband may engage in business in which he will prosper greatly. If he will submit to me a plan that seems wise and possible to my friend, Mathon, then will I gladly lend to him my savings of an entire year, that he may have an opportunity to prove that he can succeed.' Do that, I say, and if he has within him the soul to succeed, he can prove it. If he fails, he will not owe thee more than he can hope to someday repay.

"I am a gold lender, because I own more gold than I can use in my own trade. I desire my surplus gold to labor for others, and thereby earn more gold. I do not wish to take risk of losing my gold, for I have labored much and denied myself much to secure it. Therefore, I will no longer lend any of it where I am not confident that it is safe, and will be returned to me. Neither will I lend it where I am not convinced that its earnings will be promptly paid to me.

"I have told to thee, Rodan, a few of the secrets of my token chest. From them you may understand the weakness of men, and their eagerness to borrow that which they have no certain means to repay. From this, you can see how often their high hopes of the great earnings they could make, if they but had gold, are but false hopes, they have not the ability or training to fulfill.

How can I repay when ill fate pursues me?

"Thou, Rodan, now have gold, which thou shouldst put to earning more gold for thee. Thou art about to become even as I, a gold lender. If thou dost safely preserve thy treasure, it will produce liberal earnings for thee, and be a rich source of pleasure and profit during all thy days. But if thou dost let it escape from thee, it will be a source of constant sorrow and regret, as long as thy memory doth last.

"What desirest thou most of this gold in thy wallet?"

"To keep it safe."

"Wisely spoken," replied Mathon approvingly. "Thy first desire is for safety. Thinkest thou that in the custody of thy sister's husband, it would be truly safe from possible loss?"

"I fear not, for he is not wise in guarding gold."

"Then be not swayed by foolish sentiments of obligation to trust thy treasure to any person. If thou wouldst help thy family or thy friends, find other ways than risking the loss of thy treasure. Forget not that gold slippeth away in unexpected ways from those unskilled in guarding it. As well, waste thy treasure in extravagance as let others lose it for thee.

"What next, after safety, dost desire of this treasure of thine?"

"That it earn more gold."

"Again, thou speakest with wisdom. It should be made to earn and grow larger. Gold wisely lent may even double itself with its earnings before a man like you groweth old. If you risk losing it, you risk losing all that it would earn as well.

"Therefore, be not swayed by the fantastic plans of impractical men, who think they see ways to force thy gold to make earnings unusually large. Such plans are the creations of dreamers, unskilled in the safe and dependable laws of trade. Be conservative in what thou expect it to earn, that thou mayest keep and enjoy thy treasure. To hire it out with a promise of usurious returns, is to invite loss.

"Seek to associate thyself with men and enterprises whose success is established, that thy treasure may earn liberally under their skillful use, and be guarded safely by their wisdom and experience.

"Thus, mayest thou avoid the misfortunes that follow most of the sons of men to whom the gods see fit to entrust gold."

When Rodan would thank him for his wise advice, he would not listen, saying, "The king's gift shall teach thee much wisdom. If wouldst keep thy fifty pieces of gold, thou must be discreet indeed. Many uses will tempt thee. Much advice will be spoken to thee. Numerous opportunities to make large profits will be offered thee. The stories from my token box should warn thee, before thou let any piece of gold leave thy pouch to be sure that thou hast a safe way to pull it back again. Should my further advice appeal to thee, return again? It is gladly given.

"Ere thou goest, read this which I have carved beneath the lid of my token box. It applies equally to the borrower and the lender."

Better a Little Caution than a Great Regret.

Chapter VII

THE TALE OF THE WALLS OF BABYLON

*Up above, valiant defenders were
battling to hold the walls.*

THE TALE OF THE WALLS OF BABYLON

OLD BANZAR, grim warrior of another day, stood guard at the passageway leading to the top of the ancient walls of Babylon. Up above, valiant defenders were battling to hold the walls. Upon them depended the future existence of this great city with its hundreds of thousands of citizens.

Listen to Audio

Over the walls came the roar of the attacking armies, the yelling of many men, the trampling of thousands of horses, the deafening boom of the battering rams pounding the bronzed gates.

https://MoreHelp.us/C-7 →

In the street behind the gate, lounged the spearmen, awaiting to defend the entrance should the gates give way. They were but few for the task. The main armies of Babylon were with their king, far away in the east upon the great expedition against the Elamites. No attack upon the city being anticipated during their absence, the defending forces were small. Unexpectedly from the north bore down the mighty armies of the Assyrians. The walls must hold or Babylon was doomed.

About Bandar were great crowds of citizens, white faced and terrified, eagerly seeking news of the battle. With hushed awe, they viewed the stream of wounded and dead being carried, or led out of the passageway.

Here was the crucial point of attack. After three days of circling about the city, the enemy had suddenly thrown his great strength against this section and this gate.

The defenders, from the top of the wall, fought off the climbing platforms and the sealing ladders of the attackers with arrows, burning oil, and lastly spears, if any reached the top. Against the defenders, thousands of the enemies' archers poured a deadly barrage of arrows.

Old Banzar had the vantage point for news. He was closest to the conflict and first to hear of each fresh repulse of the frenzied attackers.

An elderly merchant crowded close to him, his palsied hands quivering. "Tell me! Tell me!", he pleaded. "They cannot get in. My sons are with the good king. There is no one to protect my old wife. My goods, they will steal all. My food, they will leave nothing. We are old, too old to defend ourselves—too old for slaves. We shall starve. We shall die. Tell me they cannot get in."

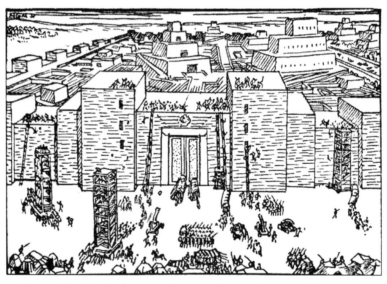

The Walls of Babylon, as they confronted an attacking army.

"Calm thyself, good merchant," the guard responded. 'The walls of Babylon are strong. Go back to the bazaar and tell your wife that the walls will protect you and all of your possessions as safely as they

106

protect the rich treasures of the king. Keep close to the walls, lest the arrows flying over, strike you!"

A woman with a babe in arms took the old man's place as he withdrew. "Sergeant, what news from the top? Tell me truly that I may reassure my poor husband. He lies with fever from his terrible wounds, yet insists upon his armor and his spear to protect me, who am with child. Terrible he says will be the vengeful lust of our enemies, should they break in.""Be thou of good heart, thou mother that is, and is again to be, the walls of Babylon will protect you and your babes. They are high and strong. Hear ye not the yells of our valiant defenders as they empty the caldrons of burning oil upon the ladder scalers?"

"Yes, that do I hear, and also the roar of the battering rams that do hammer at our gates."

"Back to thy husband. Tell him the gates are strong and withstand the rams. Also, that the scalers climb the walls but to receive the waiting spear thrust. Watch thy way and hasten behind yon buildings."

He lays with fever from his terrible wounds, yet insists upon his armor and his spear to protect me.

Bandar stepped aside to clear the passage for heavily armed reinforcements. As with clanking bronze shields and heavy tread they tramped by, a small girl plucked at his girdle.

"Tell me please, soldier, are we safe?", she pleaded. "I hear the awful noises. I see the men all bleeding. I am so frightened. What will become of our family, of my mother, little brother, and the baby?"

The grim old campaigner blinked his eyes, and thrust forward his chin as he beheld the child.

"Be not afraid, little one," he reassured her. "The walls of Babylon will protect you, and mother, and little brother, and the baby. It was for the safety of such as you, that the good Queen Semiramis built them over a hundred years ago. Never have they been broken through. Go back and tell your mother, and little brother, and the baby, that the walls of Babylon will protect them, and they need have no fear."

Day after day, old Bandar stood at his post and watched the reinforcements file up the passageway, there to stay and fight until wounded or dead they came down once more. Around him, unceasingly crowded the throngs of frightened citizens, eagerly seeking to learn if the walls would hold. To all he gave his answer with the fine dignity of an old soldier. "The walls of Babylon will protect you."

For three weeks and five days, the attack waged with scarcely ceasing violence. Harder and grimmer set the jaw of Bandar, as the passage behind, wet with the blood of the many wounded, was churned into mud by the never ceasing streams of men passing up and staggering down. Each day, the slaughtered attackers piled up in heaps before the wall. Each night, they were carried back and buried by their comrades.

Upon the fifth night of the fourth week, the clamor without diminished. The first streaks of daylight illuminating the plains, disclosed great clouds of dust raised by the retreating armies.

A mighty shout went up from the defenders. There was no mistaking its meaning. It was repeated by the waiting troops behind the walls. It was echoed by the citizens upon the streets. It swept over the city with the violence of a storm.

People rushed from the houses. The streets were jammed with a throbbing mob. The pent-up fear of weeks found an outlet in the wild chorus of joy. From the top of the high tower of the Temple of Bel burst forth the flames of victory. Skyward floated the column of blue smoke to carry the message far and wide.

The pent-up fear of weeks found an outlet
in the wild chorus of joy.

The walls of Babylon had once again repulsed a mighty and vicious foe, determined to loot her rich treasures, and to ravish and enslave her citizens.

Babylon endured century after century because it was FULLY PROTECTED. It could not afford to be otherwise.

The walls of Babylon were an outstanding example of man's need and desire for protection. This desire is inherent in the human race. It is just as strong today as it ever was, but we have developed broader and better plans to accomplish the same purpose.

In this day, behind the impregnable walls of insurance, savings accounts, and dependable investments, we can guard ourselves against the unexpected tragedies that may enter any door, and seat themselves before any fireside. We cannot afford to be without adequate protection.

NOTES: _____

_____

_____

_____

_____

_____

_____

_____

_____

_____

_____

_____

_____

_____

_____

_____

THE TALE OF THE CAMEL
TRADER OF BABYLON

*Within me surged the soul of a freeman
going back to conquer his enemies and
reward his friends.*

Chapter VIII

THE TALE OF THE CAMEL TRADER OF BABYLON

The hungrier one becomes, the clearer one's mind works, also the more sensitive one becomes to the odors of food.

For two days Tarkad, the son of Azure, had tasted no food, except two small figs purloined from over the wall of a garden, before an angry Babylonian housekeeper chased him down the street. The woman's cries still rang in his ears, and restrained his restless fingers from snatching tempting fruits from the baskets of the market women between whom he strolled.

Listen to Audio

https://MoreHelp.us/C-8 →

He paced back and forth before the eating house, hoping to meet someone he knew; someone from whom he could borrow a bit of copper, that would gain him a friendly smile and a liberal helping from the fat keeper. Without the copper, he knew how unwelcome he would be.

In his abstraction, he unexpectedly found himself face to face with the tall bony figure of Dabasir, the camel trader.

"Ha! 'Tis Tarkad, whom I have been seeking, that he might repay to me the two pieces of copper which I lent to him a moon ago, and the piece of silver which I lent to him before that. We are well met. I can make good use of the coin this very day. What say, boy? What say?"

Tarkad stuttered and his face flushed. He had little desire to encounter the outspoken Dabasir. "I am sorry, very sorry, but this day, I have not the copper nor the silver with which I could repay."

"But get it then! Surely, thou canst get a few coppers and a piece of silver to repay the generosity of an old friend of thy father, who aided thee whenst thou wast in need?"

"'Tis because ill fortune does pursue me that I cannot repay."

"Ill fortune! Wouldst blame the gods for thine own weakness. Ill fortune pursues every man who thinks more of borrowing than of repaying. Come with me, boy, while I eat. I am hungry, and I would tell thee a tale."

Tarkad flinched from the brutal frankness of Dabasir, but here at least was an invitation to enter the coveted doorway of the eating house.

*My wife returned to her father and
I decided to leave Babylon.*

Dabasir pushed him to a far corner of the room, where they seated themselves upon small rugs.

When Kauskor, the proprietor, appeared smiling, Dabasir addressed him with his usual freedom. "Fat lizard of the desert, bring to me a leg of the goat very brown with much juice and bread and all of the vegetables, for I am hungry and want much food. Do not forget my friend here. Bring to him a jug of water. Have it cooled, for the day is hot."

Tarkad's heart sank. Must he sit here and drink water while he watched this man devour an entire goat leg? He said nothing. He thought of nothing he could say.

Dabasir, however, knew no such thing as silence. Smiling and waving his hand good naturedly to the other customers, all of whom knew him, he continued.

"I did hear from a traveler just returned from Urfa of a certain rich man who has a piece of stone cut so thin that one can look through it. He put it in the window of his house to keep out the rains. It is yellow, so this traveler does relate, and he was permitted to look through it, and all the outside world looked strange and not like it really is. What say you to that, Tarkad? Thinkest all the world could look to a man a different color what it is?"

"I dare say," responded the youth, much more interested in the fat leg of goat placed before Dabasir.

"Well, I know it, for I myself have seen the world all a different color from what it really is, and the tale I am about to tell relates how I came to see it in its right color once more."

"Dabasir will tell a tale," whispered a neighboring diner to his neighbor, and dragged his rug close. Other diners brought their food and crowded in a semi-circle. They crunched noisily in the ears of Tarkad and brushed him with their meaty bones. He alone was without food. Dabasir did not offer to share with him nor even motion him to a small corner of the hard bread that was broken off and had fallen from the platter to the floor.

"The tale that I am about to tell," began Dabasir, pausing to bite a goodly chunk from the goat leg, "relates to my early life and how I came to be a camel trader. Didst anyone know that I once was a slave in Syria?"

A murmur of surprise ran through the audience to which Dabasir listened with satisfaction.

"When I was a young man," continued Dabasir, after another vicious onslaught on the goat leg, "I learned the trade of my father, the making of saddles. I worked with him in his shop, and took to myself a wife. Being young and not greatly skilled, I could earn but little, just enough to support my excellent wife in a modest way. I craved good things, which I could not afford. Soon I found that the shop keepers would trust me to pay later, even though I could not pay at the time. So, I indulged my desires, and wore fine raiment, and bought many things for my wife and my home, beyond the reach of my earnings. I paid as I could, and for a while, all went well. But in time, I discovered I could not use my earnings both to live upon and to pay my debts. Creditors began to pursue me to pay for my extravagant purchases, and my life became miserable. I borrowed from my friends, but could not repay them either. Things went from bad to worse. My wife returned to her father, and I decided to leave Babylon and seek another city, where as I thought a young man might have a chance to succeed.

"For two years, I led a restless and unsuccessful life working for caravan traders. From this, I fell in with a set of likable robbers, who scoured the desert for unarmed caravans. Such deeds were unworthy of the son of my father, but I was seeing the world through a colored stone, and did not realize to what degradation I had fallen.

"We met with success on our first trip, capturing a rich haul of gold and silks and valuable merchandise. This loot, we took to Ginir and squandered.

"The second time, we were not so fortunate. Just after we had made our capture, we were attacked by the spearmen of a native chief to whom the caravans paid for protection. Our two leaders were killed, and the rest of us were taken to Damascus, where we were stripped of our clothing and sold as slaves.

We were stripped of our clothing and sold as slaves.

"I was purchased for two pieces of silver by a Syrian desert chief. With my hair shorn and but a loin cloth to wear, I was not so different from the other slaves. Being a reckless youth, I thought it merely an adventure, until my master took me before his four wives and told them they could have me for a eunuch.

'Then, indeed, did I realize the hopelessness of my situation. These men of the desert were fierce and warlike. I was subject to their will without weapons or means of escape.

"Fearful I stood, as those four women looked me over. I wondered if I could expect pity from them. Sira, the first wife, was older than the others. Her face was impassive as she looked upon me. I turned from her with little consolation. The next was a contemptuous beauty, who gazed at me as indifferently as if I had been a worm of the earth. The two younger ones tittered as though it were all an exciting joke.

"It seemed an age that I stood waiting sentence. Each woman appeared willing for the others to decide. Finally, Sira spoke up in a cold voice.

" 'Of eunuchs we have plenty, but of camel tenders we have few, and they are a worthless lot. Even this day I would visit my mother who is sick with the fever, and there is no slave I would trust to lead my camel. Ask this slave if he can lead a camel."

"My master thereupon questioned me. 'What know you of camels?'

"Striving to conceal my eagerness, I replied, 'I can make them kneel, I can load them, I can lead them on long trips without tiring. If need be, I can repair their trappings.'

" The slave speaks forward enough,' observed my master. 'If thou so desire, Sira, take this man for thy camel tender.'

"So I was turned over to Sira, and that day I led her camel upon a long journey to her sick mother. I took the occasion to thank her for her intercession, and also to tell her that I was not a slave by birth, but the son of a freeman, an honorable saddle maker of Babylon. I also told her much of my story. Her comments were disconcerting to me, and I pondered much afterwards on what she said.

" 'How can you call yourself a free man when your weakness has brought you to this?

If a man has in himself the soul of a slave, will he not become one no matter what his birth, even as water seeks its level? If a man has within him the soul of a free man, will he not become respected and honored in his own city, in spite of his misfortune?'

"For over a year I was a slave and lived with the slaves, but I could not become as one of them. One day Sira asked me, 'In the evening time when the other slaves can mingle and enjoy the society of each other, why dost sit in thy tent alone?'

"To which I responded, 'I am pondering what you have said to me. I wonder if I have the soul of a slave. I cannot join them, so I must sit apart.'

" 'I, too, must sit apart', she confided. My dowry was large and my lord married me because of it. Yet he does not desire me. What every woman longs for is to be desired. Because of this and because I am barren and have neither son nor daughter, must I sit apart. Where I, a man, I would rather die than be such a slave, but the conventions of our tribe make slaves of women.'

" 'Have I the soul of a man, or have I the soul of a slave? What think you?', I asked.

" 'Have you a desire to repay the just debts you owe in Babylon?'

" 'Yes, I have the desire, but I see no way.'

" 'If thou contentedly let the years slip by, and make no effort to repay, then thou hast but the contemptible soul of a slave. No man is otherwise, who cannot respect himself, and no man can respect himself, who does not repay honest debts.'

" 'But what can I do, who am a slave in Syria.'

" 'Stay a slave in Syria, thou weakling."

" 'I am not a weakling', I denied hotly.

" 'Then prove it.'

" 'How?'

" 'Does not thy great king fight his enemies in every way he can, and with every force he has? Thy debts are thy enemies, that have run thee out of Babylon. You left them alone, and they grew too strong for thee. Hadst fought them as a man, thou couldst have conquered them and been one honored among thy townspeople. But thou had not the soul to fight them, and behold thou hast gone down until thou art a slave in Syria.'

"Much I thought over her unkind accusations, and many defensive phrases I worded to prove myself not a slave at heart, but I was not to have the chance to use them. Three days later, the maid of Sira took me to her mistress.

How can you call yourself a free man when your weakness has brought you to this?

" 'My mother is again very sick', she said. 'Saddle the two best camels in my husband's herd. Tie on water skins and saddle bags for a long journey. The maid will give thee food at the kitchen tent.' I

120

packed the camels, wondering much at the quantity of provisions the maid provided, for the mother dwelt less than a day's journey away. The maid rode the rear camel, which followed, and I led the camel of my mistress. When we reached her mother's house, it was just dark. Sira dismissed the maid and said to me:

" 'Hast thou the soul of a free man or the soul of a slave?

" 'The soul of a free man', I responded.

" 'Now is thy chance to prove it. Thy master hath imbibed deeply, and his chiefs are in a stupor. Take then these camels, and make thy escape. Here in this bag is raiment of thy master's to disguise thee. I will say thou stole the camels and ran away while I visited my sick mother.'

" Thou hast the soul of a queen', I told her. 'Much do I wish that I might lead thee to happiness.'

" 'Happiness', she responded, 'awaits not the runaway wife who seeks it in far lands among strange people. Go thy own way, and may the gods of the desert protect thee, for the way is far and barren of food or water.'

"I needed no further urging, but thanked her warmly and was away into the night. I knew not this strange country and had only a dim idea of the direction in which lay Babylon, but struck out bravely across the desert toward the hills. One camel I rode, and the other I led. All that night I traveled and all the next day, urged on by the knowledge of the terrible fate that was meted out to slaves who stole their master's property and tried to escape.

"Late that afternoon, I reached a rough country as uninhabitable as the desert. The sharp rocks bruised the feet of my faithful camels, and soon they were picking their way slowly and painfully along. I met neither man nor beast and could well understand why they shunned this inhospitable land.

"It was such a journey from then on, as few men live to tell of. Day after day, we plodded along. Food and water gave out. The heat of the sun was merciless. At the end of the ninth day, I slid from the back of my mount with the feeling that I was too weak to ever remount, and I would surely die, lost in this abandoned country.

"I stretched out upon the ground and slept, not waking until the first gleam of daylight.

"I sat up and looked about me. There was a coolness in the morning air. My camels lay dejected not far away. About me was a vast waste of broken country, covered with rock and sand and thorny things, no sign of water, naught to eat for man or camel.

"Could it be that in this peaceful quiet I faced my end? My mind was clearer than it had ever been before. My body now seemed of little importance. My parched and bleeding lips, my dry and swollen tongue, my empty stomach, all had lost their supreme importance of the day before.

"I looked across into the uninviting distance, and once again came to me the question, 'Have I the soul of a slave or the soul of a free man?' Then with clearness, I realized that if I had the soul of a slave, 1 should give up, lie down in the desert, and die, a fitting end for a runaway slave.

"But if I had the soul of a free man, what then? Surely, I would force my way back to Babylon, repay the people who had trusted me, bring happiness to my wife who had cared for me, bring peace and contentment to my parents.

" 'Thy debts are thine enemies who have run thee out of Babylon', Sira had said. Yes, it was so. Why had I refused to stand my ground like a man? Why had I permitted my wife to go back to her father? Why had I been weak like a slave if I had not the soul of one?

Where the determination is, the way can be found.

"Then a strange thing happened. All the world seemed to be of a different color, as though I had been looking at it through a colored stone which had suddenly been removed. At last, I saw the true values in life.

"Die in the desert! Not I! With a new vision, I saw the things that I must do. First, I would go back to Babylon and face every man to whom I owed an unpaid debt. I should tell them that after years of wandering and misfortune, I had come back to pay my debts as fast as the gods would permit. Next, I should make a home for my wife, and become a citizen of whom my parents should be proud.

"My debts were my enemies, but the men I owed were my friends, for they had trusted me and believed in me.

"I staggered weakly to my feet. What mattered hunger? What mattered thirst? They were but incidents on the road to Babylon.

Within me surged the soul of a free man, going back to conquer his enemies and reward his friends. I thrilled with the great resolve.

"The glazed eyes of my camels brightened at the new note in my husky voice. With great effort, after many attempts, they gained their feet. With pitiful perseverance, they pushed on toward the north where something within me said we would find Babylon.

"We found water. We passed into a more fertile country where were grass and fruit. We found the trail to Babylon because the soul of a free man looks at life as a series of problems to be solved and solves them, while the soul of a slave whines, 'What can I do who am but a slave?'

"How about thee, Tarkad? Dost thy empty stomach make thy head exceedingly clear? Art ready to take the road that leads to Babylon?"

Moisture came to the eyes of the youth. He rose eagerly to his knees. 'Thou hast shown me a vision; already I feel the soul of a free man surge within me."

Again Dabasir turned to his food. "Kauskor, thou snail", he called loudly to be heard in the kitchen, "the food is cold. Bring me more meat fresh from the roasting. Bring thou also a portion for Tarkad, the son of my old friend, who is hungry and shall eat with me."

So ended the tale of Dabasir, the camel trader of old Babylon. He found his own soul, when he realized a great truth, a truth that had been known and used by wise men long before his time.

It has led men of all ages out of difficulties and into success, and it will continue to do so for those who have the wisdom to understand its magic power. It is for any man to use who reads these lines.

Where the Determination is, the Way Can Be Found

THE TALE OF THE CLAY TABLETS FROM BABYLON

*One expects the dim and distant past to
speak of romance and adventure.*

Chapter IX

THE TALE OF THE CLAY TABLETS FROM BABYLON

St. Swithin's College
Nottingham University
Newark-On-Trent
Nottingham

Listen to Audio

https://MoreHelp.us/C-9 →

October 21, 1934

Professor Franklin Caldwell,
Care of British Scientific Expedition,
Hillah, Mesopotamia

My Dear Professor:

The five clay tablets from your recent excavation in the ruins of Babylon arrived on the same boat with your letter. I have been fascinated no end, and have spent many pleasant hours translating their inscriptions. I should have answered your letter at once but delayed until I could complete the translations which are attached.

The tablets arrived without damage, thanks to your careful use of preservatives and excellent packing.

You will be as astonished as we in the laboratory, at the story they relate. One expects the dim and distant past to speak of romance and adventure. "Arabian Nights" sort of things, you know. When instead it discloses the problem of a person named Dabasir, to pay off his debts, one realizes that conditions upon this old world have not changed as much in five thousand years as one might expect.

It's odd, you know, but these old inscriptions rather 'rag' me, as the students say. Being a college professor, I am supposed to be a thinking human being possessing a working knowledge upon most subjects. Yet, here comes this old chap out of the dust-covered ruins of Babylon to offer a way, I had never heard of, to pay off my debts and at the same time acquire gold to jingle in my wallet.

Pleasant thought, I say, and interesting to prove whether it will work as well nowadays as it did in old Babylon. Mrs. Shrewsbury and myself are planning to try out his plan upon our own affairs which could be much improved.

Wishing you the best of luck in your worthy undertaking and waiting eagerly another opportunity to assist, I am.

Yours sincerely,

Alfred H. Shrewsbury,
Department of Archaeology

TABLET No. I

Therefore, do I here engrave the name of
every man to whom I am indebted.

Now when the moon becometh full I, Dabasir, who am but recently returned from slavery in Syria, with the determination to pay my many just debts, and become a man of means worthy of respect in my native city of Babylon, do here engrave upon the clay, a permanent record of my affairs to guide and assist me in carrying through my high desires.

Under the wise advice of my good friend Mathon, the gold lender, I am determined to follow an exact plan that he doth say will lead any honorable man out of debt into means and self-respect.

This plan includeth three purposes which are my hope and desire.

First, the PLAN doth provide for my future prosperity.

Therefore, one-tenth of all I earn shall be set aside as my own to keep. For Mathon speaketh wisely when he saith:
"That man who keepeth in his purse both gold and silver that he need not spend, is good to his family and loyal to his king.

"The man who hath but a few coppers in his purse, is indifferent to his family and indifferent to his king.

"But the man who hath naught in his purse, is unkind to his family and is disloyal to his king, for his own heart is bitter.

"Therefore, the man who wisheth to achieve, must have coin that he may keep to jingle in his purse, that he have in his heart love for his family and loyalty to his king."

Second, the PLAN doth provide that I shall support and clothe my good wife, who hath returned to me with loyalty from the house of her father. For Mathon doth say that to take good care of a faithful wife, putteth self-respect into the heart of a man and addeth strength and determination to his purposes.

Therefore seven-tenths of all I earn shall be used to provide a home, clothes to wear, and food to eat, with a bit extra to spend, that our lives be not lacking in pleasure and enjoyment. But he doth further enjoin the greatest care, that we spend not greater than seven-tenths of what I earn for these worthy purposes. Herein lieth the success of the PLAN. I must live upon this portion and never use more nor buy what I may not pay for out of this portion.

TABLET No. II

*Alkahad, the house owner, was indeed disagreeable
and insisted that he would make me trouble.*

Third, the PLAN doth provide that out of my earnings my debts shall
be paid.

Therefore each time the moon is full, two-tenths of all I have earned
shall be divided honorably and fairly among those who have trusted
me and to whom I am indebted. Thus, in due time will all my
indebtedness be surely paid.

Therefore, do I here engrave the names of every man to whom I am
indebted and the honest amount of my debt.

> Fahru, the cloth weaver, 2 silver, 6 copper.
> Sinjar, the couch maker, 1 silver.
> Ahmar, my friend, 3 silver, 1 copper.
> Zankar, my friend, 4 silver, 7 copper.
> Askanir, my friend, 1 silver, 3 copper.
> Harinsir, the jewelmaker, 6 silver, 2 copper.
> Diarbeker, my father's friend, 4 silver, 1 copper.
> Alkahad, the house owner, 14 silver.

Mathon, the gold lender, 9 silver.
Birejik, the farmer, 1 silver, 7 copper.

(From here on, disintegrated. Cannot be deciphered.)

NOTES: _____

_____

_____

_____

_____

_____

_____

_____

_____

_____

_____

_____

_____

_____

_____

_____

_____

_____

_____

_____

_____

_____

_____

_____

TABLET No. III

*I intercepted a fine herd of camels and
bought many sound ones.*

To these creditors do I owe in total one hundred and nineteen pieces of silver and one hundred and forty-one pieces of copper. Because I did owe these sums and saw no way to repay, in my folly, I didst permit my wife to return to her father, and didst leave my native city and seek easy wealth elsewhere, only to find disaster and to see myself sold into the degradation of slavery.

Now that Mathon doth show me how I can repay my debts in small sums out of my earnings, do I realize the great extent of my folly in running away from the results of my extravagances.

Therefore, have I visited my creditors and explained to them that I have no resources with which to pay except my ability to earn, and that I intend to apply two-tenths of all I earn upon my indebtedness, evenly and honestly. This much can I pay but no more. Therefore, if they be patient, in time, my obligations will be paid in full.

Ahmar, whom I thought my best friend, reviled me bitterly and I left him in humiliation. Birejik, the farmer, pleaded that I pay him first as he didst badly need help. Alkahad, the house-owner, was indeed disagreeable and insisted that he would make me trouble unless I didst soon settle in full with him.

All the rest willingly accepted my proposal. Therefore, am I more determined than ever to carry through, being convinced that it is easier to pay one's just debts than to avoid them. Even though I cannot meet the needs and demands of a few of my creditors I will deal impartially with all.

NOTES: _____

_____

_____

_____

_____

_____

_____

_____

_____

_____

_____

_____

_____

_____

_____

_____

_____

_____

_____

_____

TABLET No. IV

Again the moon shines full. I have worked hard with a free mind. My good wife hath supported my intentions to pay my creditors. Because of our wise determination, I have earned during the past moon, buying camels of sound wind and good legs, for Nebatur, the sum of nineteen pieces of silver.

This I have divided according to the PLAN. One-tenth have I set aside to keep as my own, seven-tenths have I divided with my good wife to pay for our living. Two-tenths have I divided among my creditors as evenly as could be done in coppers.

I did not see Ahmar, but left it with his wife. Birejik was so pleased he would kiss my hand. Old Alkahad alone was grouchy, and said I must pay faster. To which I replied that if I were permitted to be well fed and not worried, that alone would enable me to pay faster. All the others thanked me and spoke well of my efforts.

Therefore, at the end of one moon, my indebtedness is reduced by almost four pieces of silver and I possess almost two pieces of silver besides, upon which no man hath claim. My heart is lighter than it hath been for a long time.

Again, the moon shines full. I have worked hard, but with poor success. Few camels have I been able to buy. Only eleven pieces of silver have I earned. Nevertheless, my good wife and I have stood by the plan even though we have bought no new raiment and eaten little but herbs. Again, I paid ourselves one-tenth of the eleven pieces, while we lived upon seven-tenths. I was surprised when Ahmar commended my payment, even though small. So did Birejik. Alkahad flew into a rage, but when told to give back his portion if he did not wish it, he became reconciled. The others as before were content.

Again the moon shines full, and I am greatly rejoiced. I intercepted a fine herd of camels and bought many sound ones. Therefore, my earnings were forty-two pieces of silver. This moon, my wife and myself have bought much needed sandals and raiment. Also, we have dined well on meat and fowl.

More than eight pieces of silver we have paid to our creditors. Even Alkahad did not protest.

Great is the PLAN, for it leadeth us out of debt and giveth us wealth which is ours to keep.

Three times the moon hath been full since I last carved upon this clay. Each time, I paid to myself one-tenth of all I earned. Each time, my good wife and I have lived upon seven-tenths, even though at times it was difficult. Each time, have I paid to my creditors two-tenths.

In my purse, I now have twenty-one pieces of silver that is mine. It maketh my head to stand straight upon my shoulders, and maketh me proud to walk among my friends.

My wife keepeth well our home and is becomingly gowned. We are happy to live together.

The PLAN is of untold value. Hath it not made an honorable man of an ex-slave.

TABLET No. V

Again the moon shines full, and I remember that it is long since I carved upon the clay. Twelve moons in truth have come and gone. But this day, I will not neglect my record, because upon this day I have paid the last of my debts. This is the day upon which my good wife and my thankful self, celebrate with great feasting, that our determination hath been achieved.

Many things occurred upon my final visit to my creditors that I shall long remember. Ahmar begged my forgiveness, for his unkind words, and said that I was one of all others he most desired for a friend.

Old Alkahad is not so bad after all, for he said, "Thou wert once a piece of soft clay to be pressed and molded by any hand that touched thee, but now thou art a piece of bronze, capable of holding an edge. If thou needst silver or gold at any time, come to me."

Nor is he the only one who holdeth me in high regard. Many others speak deferentially to me. My good wife looketh upon me with a light in her eyes that doth make a man have confidence in himself.

Yet, it is the PLAN that hath made my success. It hath enabled me to pay all my debts and to jingle both gold and silver in my purse. I do commend it to all who wish to get ahead. For truly if it will enable an ex-slave to pay his debts and have gold in his purse, will it not aid any man to find independence? Nor am I, myself, finished with it, for I am convinced that if I follow it further, it will make me rich among men.

St. Swithin's College
Nottingham University
Newark-On-Trent
Nottingham

November 7, 1936

Professor Franklin Caldwell,
Care of British Scientific Expedition,
Hillah, Mesopotamia

My Dear Professor:

If, in your further digging into those bally ruins of Babylon, you encounter the ghost of a former resident, an old camel trader named Dabasir, do me a favor. Tell him that his scribbling upon those clay tablets, so long ago, has earned for him the life-long gratitude of a couple of college folks back here in England.

You will possibly remember my writing a year ago, that Mrs. Shrewsbury and myself intended to try his plan for getting out of debt, and at the same time having gold to jingle. You may have guessed, even though we tried to keep from our friends, our desperate straits.

We were frightfully humiliated for years by a lot of old debts, and worried sick for fear some of the tradespeople might start a scandal that would force me out of the college. We paid and paid—every shilling we could squeeze out of income, but it was hardly enough to hold things even. Besides we were forced to do all our buying where we could get further credit regardless of higher costs.

It developed into one of those vicious circles that grow worse instead of better. Our struggles were getting hopeless. We could not move to less costly rooms because we owed the landlord. There did not appear to be anything we could do to improve our situation.

Then, here comes your acquaintance, the old camel trader from Babylon, with a plan to do just what we wished to accomplish. He jolly well stirred us up to follow his system. We made a list of all our debts, and I took it around and showed it to everyone we owed.

I explained how it was simply impossible for me to ever pay them the way things were going along. They could readily see this themselves from the figures. Then I explained that the only way I saw to pay in full, was to set aside twenty percent of my income each month to be divided pro rata, which would pay them in full in a little over two years. That, in the meantime, we would go on a cash basis, and give them the further benefit of our cash purchases.

They were really quite decent. Our greengrocer, a wise old chap, put it in a way that helped to bring around the rest. "If you pay for all you buy, and then pay some on what you owe, that is better than you have done, for ye ain't paid down the account none in three years."

Finally I secured all their names to an agreement, binding them not to molest us, as long as the twenty percent of income was paid regularly. Then we began scheming on how to live upon seventy percent. We were determined to keep that extra ten percent to jingle. The thought of silver and possibly gold was most alluring.

It was like having an adventure to make the change. We enjoyed figuring this way and that, to live comfortably upon that remaining seventy percent. Started with rent and managed to secure a fair reduction. Next, we put our favorite brands of tea and such under suspicion and were agreeably surprised how often we could purchase superior qualities at less cost.

It is too long a story for a letter, but anyhow it did not prove difficult. We managed, and right cheerfully at that. What a relief it proved to have our affairs in such a shape we were no longer persecuted by past due accounts.

I must not neglect, however, to tell you about that extra ten percent we were supposed to jingle. Well, we did jingle it for some time. Now don't laugh too soon. You see, that is the sporty part. It is the real fun, to start accumulating money that you do not want to spend. There is more pleasure in running up such a surplus than there could be in spending it.

After we had jingled to our hearts content, we found a more profitable use for it. We took up an investment, upon which we could pay that ten percent each month. This is proving to be the most satisfying part of our regeneration. It is the first thing we pay out of my check.

There is a most gratifying sense of security to know our investment is growing steadily. By the time my teaching days are over, it should be a snug sum, large enough so the income will take care of us from then on.

All this out of my same old check. Difficult to believe, yet absolutely true. All our old debts being gradually paid, and at the same time our investment increasing. Besides, we get along, financially, even better than before. Who would believe there could be such a difference in results between following a financial plan and just drifting along.

At the end of the next year, when all our old bills shall have been paid, we will have more to pay upon our investment, besides some extra for travel. We are determined never again to permit our living expenses to exceed seventy percent of our income.

Now you can understand why we would like to extend our personal thanks to that old chap, whose plan saved us from our 'Hell on Earth', DEBTS.

He knew. He had been through it all. He wanted others to benefit from his own bitter experiences. That is why he spent tedious hours carving his message upon the clay.

He had a real message for fellow sufferers, a message so important, that after five thousand years, it has risen out of the ruins of Babylon, just as true and just as vital as the day it was buried.

Yours sincerely,

Alfred H. Shrewsbury,
Department of Archaeology

NOTES: _____

_____

_____

_____

_____

_____

_____

_____

_____

_____

_____

_____

_____

_____

_____

_____

_____

_____

_____

_____

_____

_____

_____

_____

_____

_____

_____

_____

_____

_____

_____

_____

_____

HISTORICAL SKETCH OF BABYLON

THE WINGED BULL OF BABYLON

Symbolizing
The Intelligence of Man
The Speed of the Bird
The Strength of the Bull

Chapter X

Historical Sketch of Babylon

The Hanging Gardens of Babylon.

Historical Sketch of Babylon

In the pages of history, there lives no city more glamorous than Babylon. Its very name conjures visions of wealth and splendor. Its treasures of gold and jewels were fabulous. One naturally pictures such a wealthy city as located in a suitable setting of tropical luxuriance, surrounded by rich natural resources of forests and mines. Such was not the case. It was located beside the Euphrates River, in a flat, arid valley. It had no forests, no mines— not even stone for building. It was not even located upon a natural trade route. The rainfall was insufficient to raise crops.

Babylon is an outstanding example of man's ability to achieve great objectives, using whatever means are at his disposal. All of the resources supporting this large city were man-developed. All of its riches were man-made.

Listen to Audio

https://MoreHelp.us/C-10 →

Babylon possessed just two natural resources—a fertile soil and water in the river. With one of the greatest engineering accomplishments of this or any other day, Babylonian engineers diverted the waters from the river by means of dams and immense irrigation canals. Far out across that arid valley went these canals to pour the life-giving waters over the fertile soil. This ranks among the first engineering feats known to history. Such abundant crops as were the reward of this irrigation system here, we doubt if the world had ever seen before.

Fortunately, during its long existence, Babylon was ruled by successive lines of kings to whom conquest and plunder were but incidental. While it engaged in many wars, most of these were local or defensive against ambitious conquerors from other countries who coveted the fabulous 'Treasures of Babylon". The outstanding rulers of Babylon live in history because of their wisdom, enterprise, and justice. Babylon produced no strutting monarchs who sought to conquer the known world, that all nations might pay homage to their egotism.

As a city, Babylon exists no more. When those energizing human forces that built and maintained the city for thousands of years, were withdrawn, it soon became a deserted ruin. The site of the city is in Asia about six hundred miles east of the Suez Canal, just north of the Persian Gulf. The latitude is about 30 degrees above the Equator, practically the same as that of Yuma, Arizona. It possessed a climate similar to that of this American city, hot and dry.

Today, this valley of the Euphrates, once a populous irrigated farming district, is again the wind-swept arid waste. Scant grass and desert shrubs strive for existence against the wind-blown sands. Gone are the fertile fields, the mammoth cities, and the long caravans of rich merchandise. Nomadic bands of Arabs, securing a scant living by tending small herds, are the only inhabitants. Such it has been since about the beginning of the Christian era.

Dotting this valley are earthen hills. For centuries, they were considered by travelers to be nothing else. The attention of archaeologists were finally attracted to them, because of broken pieces of pottery and brick washed down by the occasional rain storms. Expeditions, financed by European and American Museums, were sent here to excavate and see what could be found. Picks and shovels soon proved these hills to be ancient cities. City graves, they might well be called.

Babylon was one of these. Over it, for something like twenty centuries, the winds had scattered the desert dust. Built originally of brick, all exposed walls had disintegrated and gone back to earth once more. Such is Babylon, the wealthy city, today. A heap of dirt, so long abandoned that no living person even knew its name until it was discovered by carefully removing the refuse of centuries from the streets and the fallen wreckage of its noble temples and palaces.

Many scientists consider the civilization of Babylon and other cities in this valley to be the oldest of which there is a definite record. Positive dates have been proved reaching back 8000 years. An interesting fact in this connection, is the means used to determine these dates. Uncovered in the ruins of Babylon were descriptions of an eclipse of the sun. Modern astronomers readily computed the time when such an eclipse, visible in Babylon, occurred, and thus established a known relationship between their calendar and our own.

In this way, we have proved that 8,000 years ago the Sumerites, who inhabited Babylonia, were living in walled cities. One can only conjecture for how many centuries previous such cities had existed. Their inhabitants were not mere barbarians living within protecting walls. They were an educated and enlightened people. So far, as written history goes, they were the first engineers, the first astronomers, the first mathematicians, the first financiers, and the first people to have a written language.

Irrigation Canal of Babylon.

147

Mention has already been made of the irrigation systems which transformed the arid valley into an agricultural paradise. The remains of these canals can still be traced, although they are mostly filled with accumulated sand. Some of them were of such size that, when empty of water, a dozen horses could be ridden along their bottoms abreast. In size, they compare favorably with the largest canals in Colorado and Utah.

In addition to irrigating the valley lands, Babylonian engineers completed another project of similar magnitude. By means of an elaborate drainage system, they reclaimed an immense area of swamp land at the mouths of the Euphrates and Tigris Rivers, and put this also under cultivation.

Herodotus, the Greek traveler and historian, visited Babylon while it was in its prime, and has given us the only known description by an outsider. His writings give a graphic description of the city and some of the unusual customs of its people. He mentions the remarkable fertility of the soil and the bountiful harvests of wheat, barley, and emmer which they produced.

The glory of Babylon has faded, but its wisdom has been preserved for us. For this, we are indebted to their form of records. In that distant day, the use of paper had not been invented. Instead, they laboriously engraved their writing upon tablets of moist clay. When completed, these were baked and became hard tile. In size, they were about six by eight inches and an inch in thickness.

These clay tablets, as they are commonly called, were used much as we use modern forms of writing. Upon them were engraved lengthy legends, rare poetry, history, transcriptions of royal decrees, the laws of the lands, titles to property, promissory notes and even letters which were dispatched by messengers to distant cities. From these clay tablets, we are permitted an insight into the intimate personal affairs of the people. For example, one tablet, evidently from the records of a country storekeeper, relates that upon the given date, a certain named customer brought in a cow and exchanged it for seven sacks of wheat, three being delivered at the time and the other four to await the customer's pleasure.

Another gives a part of the autobiography of Ashurbanipal, one of their kings. Among other things, he advises us: "The beautiful writing in Sumerian, that is difficult to remember, it was my joy to repeat. I directed the weaving of reed shields and breastworks like a pioneer. I had the learning that all clerks of every kind possess when their time of maturity comes. At the same time, I learned what is proper for lordship."

Safely buried in the wrecked cities, archaeologists have recovered entire libraries of these tablets, hundreds of thousands of them.

One of the outstanding wonders of Babylon, was the immense walls surrounding the city. The ancients ranked them with the great pyramid of Egypt as belonging to the "Seven Wonders of the world". Queen Semiramis is credited with having erected the first walls during the early history of the city. Modern excavators have been unable to find any trace of the original walls. Nor is their exact height known. From mention made by early writers, it is estimated they were about fifty to sixty feet high, faced on the outer side with burnt brick and further protected by a deep moat of water.

The later and more famous walls were started about six hundred years before the time of Christ by King Nabopolassar. Upon such a gigantic scale did he plan the rebuilding, he did not live to see the work finished. This was left to his son, Nebuchadnezzar, whose name is familiar in Biblical history.

The height and length of these later walls staggers belief. They are reported upon reliable authority to have been about one hundred and sixty feet high, the equivalent of the height of a modern fifteen story office building. The total length is estimated as between nine and eleven miles. So wide was the top, that a six-horse chariot could be driven around them. Of this tremendous structure, little now remains except portions of the foundations and the moat. In addition to the ravages of the elements, the Arabs completed the destruction by quarrying the brick for building purposes elsewhere.

Against the walls of Babylon marched, in turn, the victorious armies of almost every victorious conqueror of that age of wars of conquest. A host of kings laid siege to Babylon, but always in vain. Invading armies of that day were not to be considered lightly. Historians speak of such units as 10,000 horsemen, 25,000 chariots, 1200 regiments of foot soldiers, with 1000 men to the regiment. Often two to three years of preparation would be required to assemble war materials and depots of food along the proposed line of march.

The city of Babylon was organized much like a modern city. There were streets and shops. Peddlers offered their wares through residential districts. Priests officiated in magnificent temples. Within the city was an inner enclosure for the royal palaces. The walls about this were said to have been higher than those about the city.

The Babylonians were skilled in the arts. These included: sculpture, painting, weaving, gold working, and the manufacture of metal weapons and agricultural implements. Their jewelers created most artistic jewelry. Many samples have been recovered from the graves of its wealthy citizens and are now on exhibition in the leading museums of the world.

At a very early period, when the rest of the world was still hacking at trees with stone-headed axes, or hunting and fighting with flint-pointed spears and arrows, the Babylonians were using axes, spears and arrows with metal heads.

The Babylonians were clever financiers and traders. So far as we know, they were the original inventors of money as a means of exchange, of promissory notes, and written titles to property.

The Ruins of Babylon.

Babylon was never entered by hostile armies until about 540 years before the birth of Christ. Even then, the walls were not captured. The story of the fall of Babylon is most unusual. Cyrus, one of the great conquerors of that period, intended to attack the city, hoped to take its impregnable walls. Advisors of Nabonidus, the King of Babylon, persuaded him to go forth to meet Cyrus and give him battle without waiting for the city to be besieged.

In the succeeding battle, Cyrus administered such an astounding defeat to the Babylonian army, it fled away from the city. Cyrus, there upon, entered the open gates and took possession without resistance.

Thereafter, the power and prestige of the city gradually waned until, in the course of a few hundred years, it was eventually abandoned, deserted, left for the winds and storms to level once again to that desert earth from which its grandeur had originally been built.

Babylon had fallen, never to rise again, but to it civilization owes much.

> ### *The eons of time have crumbled to dust the proud walls of its temples, but the wisdom of Babylon endureth.*

Part – 2

NEW UNDERSTANDING

"With a new understanding we shall find honorable ways to accomplish our desires."

Chapter XI

How to Study for Financial Success

Financial education offers definite and profitable rewards. Numerous readers of **"Gold Ahead"** have reported unexpected, and valuable results from things learned which they had the opportunity to use at once to their financial betterment.

Such results are important. They show that the clearer our insight, the better we take advantage of our opportunities. But, after all, far greater results will come later. Such knowledge can be carried through life, always available to help promote the owner's financial welfare.

Listen to Audio

https://MoreHelp.us/C-11 →

Plans of study recommended for self-development groups, school and college classes, families and individuals follow. A detailed study of each tale with the questions prepared for this purpose is recommended.

NOTES: _____

_____

_____

_____

_____

_____

_____

_____

_____

_____

PLAN OF STUDY FOR GROUPS AND CLASSES

The initial lesson should comprise the reading aloud of the first tale, "THE MAN WHO DESIRED MUCH GOLD". Next, the members of the class should be asked for examples of worthwhile men or women who were in similar situations of frustration. Or, the problems in the following section can be used for discussion.

For subsequent lessons, a certain number of questions should be allotted for which the class members would prepare written answers for the next lesson. These answers can be read and commented upon. The open forum type of class study is suggested.

This procedure can be followed through the book. Each tale can easily supply material for a number of lessons. Students, in addition to supplying answers for the questions, should be urged to bring to the class examples of financial questions for discussion. Such questions should preferably be along the same line as the theme of the tale being studied.

The older members of a class can usually supply interesting instructive experiences of their own. The younger members should be urged to consult members of their family or older acquaintances and friends for examples. The telling and discussing of these actual examples will stimulate the class to develop an analytical understanding and a clearer insight into their personal finances.

NOTES: _____

_____

_____

_____

_____

_____

_____

PLAN OF STUDY FOR INDIVIDUALS

For those who study by themselves, the following plan is recommended. First, read the preceding portion of the book the same as you would any book. Next, take up the tales in sequence, beginning with the first and study them, one at a time, as if they were lessons.

Choose a time when not tired or hurried and read the tale to be studied leisurely and thoughtfully. As you read, think whether any parts of it apply to your own affairs, or to those of members of your family or acquaintances.

After reading the one tale, secure a pencil and paper. Then turn to the question section and write out answers to some of the questions. Do not hurry. Answer each question thoughtfully, taking not more than three to five at one sitting. Several days or a week is not too long for each tale. An hour each evening should provide ample time.

Each tale is a link in a definite chain of developed thought. Therefore, best results will accrue from answering the first question as a starter and continuing in sequence on through.

Try and learn the lessons of each tale so thoroughly they will become a permanent and practical part of your working knowledge. Turn them over in your mind at other times. Look for examples in real life that may be similar.

After the study of all the tales has been completed, a review a month or so later will be found surprisingly interesting. This may be done by re-reading the entire book or by working over the questions, preferably by doing both. The student will be gratified, in making reviews, at the rapid development of a new ability to understand financial matters. Herein lies the greatest value of making a thorough study of the book, the training in logical, constructive thinking which permits the viewing of his own money affairs from the viewpoint of a practical financier.

NOTES: _____

_____

_____

_____

_____

_____

_____

_____

_____

_____

_____

_____

_____

_____

_____

_____

_____

_____

_____

_____

_____

_____

_____

_____

_____

_____

_____

_____

PLAN OF STUDY FOR FAMILIES

Every family group has a common interest in the family income. It must supply a place to live, food, clothing, and other incidentals necessary to the health and happiness of each member.

A study of the tales and the questions following can do much to give every member of the family a true understanding of the limits of available money; how it must be apportioned fairly and the advantages of not only living within the family income but building up a surplus.

High School and College students can be interested in this joint study. It is also surprising how much the younger children will learn and understand. The plan of study recommended is: first, for each member of the family to read the book; this, to be followed by group study of the questions.

In preparation for study, a certain number of questions should be allotted as a lesson. Each member of the family should write out his own answers. The reading aloud of the tale to be discussed can be done by the younger members, followed by reading the answers and their discussion. The interest of the junior members can be stimulated by allotting to them the task of compiling the monthly cost of such items as food, automobile, picture shows, car fare, etc.

NOTES: _____

_____

_____

_____

_____

_____

_____

_____

HOW TO ANALYZE
FINANCIAL PROBLEMS

*"Forget not the rich men of Nineveh
who would take no chance of losing
their principal or tying it up in
unprofitable investments."*

Chapter XII

How to Analyze Financial Problems

"For of all sad words of tongue or pen, the saddest are these: It might have been!" WHITTIER

Numerous readers of this book have written to express regrets that they had not owned a copy at times in the past when its teachings would have aided them to avoid serious losses.

If one were to drag out "the skeletons in the closet" of most families and business concerns, they would discover that a large portion of such skeletons were of financial origin.

Listen to Audio

https://MoreHelp.us/C-12 →

"Sad words" refers with a sting, to good money gone because of such financial indiscretions as, notes endorsed as an accommodation which the endorser was compelled to pay; loans to friends and others in difficulties, ignored when better times arrived; investments recommended by trusted acquaintances as absolutely sound, which proved quite the contrary; family inheritances dissipated by inside members without distribution—but why go on?

Businesses find just as many ways to commit financial indiscretions as individuals, and pay for them even more dearly.

When we have in our possession a sum of money that is ours because we have earned it or for other reasons, we have the right to decide for ourselves what disposition we wish to make of it. We can blow it upon one grand good time, go around the world, or something else we want to do. We can let it slip away for this and that, inconsequential of only temporary interest. But we hate to be over persuaded to invest in something that does not really interest us, to make loans we would prefer not to make or to have our money taken away from us under duress or misrepresentation.

If we wish to retain our capital sum, to make it grow to a treasure worthwhile in the years ahead, then it behooves us to give careful thought before doing anything with it. People are letting their savings get away from them, be taken away from them or slip away from them every day without benefit or satisfaction.

The following three problems are submitted to show how such things should be studied before action is taken.

As you read these examples, try and recall similar propositions and their outcome. Get the knack of finding the weak spots in any financial proposition. Learn to rationalize your viewpoint and not let your hopes and wishes misguide you. When such things come up to you for a decision, write them out the way these problems are presented. Then write down everything you can think of against the proposition. Upon another sheet write everything you can think of in its favor. By careful thinking you can save yourself from making such mistakes as your own father probably has made, that is if he is like most of our fathers who learned their financial knowledge by paying for it with large sums of hard-earned money. Experience is a forceful teacher but a mighty expensive one. We can learn the same truths and keep our money if we will appreciate the value of the experiences of others and make use of them for ourselves.

NOTES: _____

_____

_____

_____

PROBLEM NO. 1

The Printer and the Promoter

A printer operating a small shop secured an order to print an edition of expensive booklets from a man operating under a corporation name to sell small tracts of land out of a larger tract he had subdivided. This order amounted to $2200.00, the largest contract this printer had ever secured, and he expected to make a profit of $500.00. After securing the contract, he realized that he lacked sufficient money to pay for the extra help required and a large enough line of credit to purchase the necessary paper. He knew little about his customer, except that a few small jobs done previously had been paid promptly. He decided, quite wisely, to explain his position to the customer, and ask an advance of a part of the purchase price to be paid as the work progressed to cover the cost of paper and extra labor. The customer replied that he was accustomed to do things in a big way, and if the printer could not take care of his requirements, he would be compelled to go elsewhere.

At this point, we come to the problem. The printer thought the only problem was to find ways of getting out the order and make the profit of $500.00. The real problem, however, was whether the customer was entitled to a credit of $2200. Subsequent developments showed that the customer was operating upon a shoestring. He had an agreement with the owner of the land to sell it and collect a commission on his sales. He had little tangible property aside from the furnishings in his impressive office. He desired the printer to advance the cost of expensive sales literature so he could make a splurge with his advertising—in other words, he wished to use the printer's capital. He knew quite well that if he went to a larger printing company, their experienced credit manager would insist upon a substantial cash payment with the balance due when the booklets were delivered.

Had the printer looked at his problems from the following angle, he would have been in a position to protect himself.

A. Any person or firm expecting a credit for a substantial sum, should expect either to pay as the work progressed or supply bank or other references as to their financial responsibility.

B. The person or firm that is financially responsible never feels insulted or acts high handed if asked for credit references or advance payments.

C. How much could he lose if the account was not paid? It was, of course, $1700.00. He was betting a possible profit of $500.00 against a possible loss of over three times that amount.

This is a typical example of the shrewd speculator operating upon other peoples' capital. His pose as being such a big operator impressed the printer to such an extent that the latter borrowed the money to complete the job, which was never paid for and left him deeply in debt.

The moral to this problem is that we must not take for granted the other fellow's responsibility. Banks loan money freely to customers who have established their responsibility, but not to others. Services and materials such as a printer supplies are the equivalent of money and need just as careful guarding.

NOTES: _____

_____

_____

_____

PROBLEM No. 2

The Dentist and his Brother-in-Law

A dentist was asked by his sister and her husband to loan them $2000 to buy a small business. The brother-in-law, an accountant, capable and a good fellow all around, had lost his position and after many months of searching had been unable to secure another. The dentist was anxious to see them get a new start as they were getting into a desperate state financially, but had to tell them that he did not have that much money and was having a very hard time just then as some buildings he owned were vacant and it was difficult to raise money for taxes and payments on mortgages he owed.

The brother-in-law, knowing something about financing, visited the dentist's banker and found that the bank was willing to loan the $2000 direct to the brother-in-law, providing the dentist would endorse the note. So, he returned to the dentist and assured him that this was an easy way to put him back on his feet. He would repay the bank $75 each month from the income of the new business— thus the debt would soon be paid without any trouble or worry on the part of the dentist.

Here are the things the dentist should have considered before agreeing to the proposition.

A. If his brother-in-law could not make enough profit from the business to pay the bank as agreed in addition to the living expenses of his family, then he would be called upon to pay the bank.

B. Was the brother-in-law the sort to make a go of a business. Was a man of his ability in his own line who lacked the push to find himself a new job liable to prove more successful in an untried line of work?

C. What did he, the dentist, stand to lose? All of these, the $2000 at the bank with accrued interest, a break in pleasant family relations. Also, in case the brother-in-law did not make good, he would be more discouraged and helpless than before.

Here we have an example of those difficult, inter-family affairs that are so apt to confront the thrifty, hardworking members. They are always charged with emotional tie-ups. In this case, the worst happened as it is so apt to do in such cases. Perhaps had the dentist, on a counter proposition offered to advance a few hundred dollars, it would have helped the brother-in-law find a suitable position in his own line while the loan would have been small enough to be paid off out of the earnings of a salaried man.

NOTES: _____

_____

_____

_____

_____

_____

_____

_____

_____

_____

_____

_____

_____

_____

_____

_____

PROBLEM No. 3

The Farmer and the Gold Mine

A farmer living in Missouri, received $3000 in settlement of a relative's estate. About the same time, the mail brought him some most enticing letters and illustrated literature concerning a western gold mine.

From the literature, it seemed that for many years an old recluse of a miner had owned a mine from which, whenever he needed money, he would sell very high-grade gold ore. He was an odd old fellow and would not sell his mine or let others lease it, saying that he could have all the money he needed by just going in and digging out a few wheelbarrows of ore, so why should he be bothered by selling it, it was better than any bank. After his death, the present owners secured possession and now a company was offering stock to raise money to take out and sell the vast treasures the mine was supposed to contain.

This farmer had always worked long, hard hours. He was anxious to make a lot of money in an easy way. This story of the mine aroused his imagination. He would like to get into something like that which would make him independent. He knew that if he consulted his banker, that individual would try to discourage him and keep him from accepting this unusual opportunity, so he put his $3000, three one-thousand-dollar bills, into an envelope and mailed it to the mining company. In return, he received a handsomely lithographed stock certificate.

Here we find the typical GET-RICH-QUICK appeal which clever promoters are constantly making to the inexperienced. There are many variations, it may be an unclaimed estate, a new oil field, or innumerable other propositions which lend themselves to dramatic presentation. Let us look behind the scene at this gold mine. Yes, an old recluse had owned it for many years and often sold sacks of rich ore. It was right beside a large producing mine in which the stock paid big dividends. What the literature did not state was that the present owners had tried hard to find where the rich ore had been coming from but could not. In fact, there had been rumors at various times about this rich ore which said it was being stolen from the big mine by the miners employed there and the old man was acting as a fence to sell it. Not finding ore or any indications of it, the owners had been glad to lease the property for a nominal sum to the promoters who were selling stock, not in the mine but in their lease which gave them the option to buy at a high price if they should find ore. So, this was what the hard-working farmer, who wanted to make money easily, was investing in, a lease on a probably barren piece of property.

Here are the points which the farmer should have considered before acting so rashly with his money.

A. If this mine was as rich in gold as the circular claimed, why should he, a stranger, be offered an interest? Could not the owners have easily borrowed money to develop it without letting go an interest?

B. Would he consider buying anything as expensive with which he was familiar without an examination? For example, a herd of cattle, another forty acres of farm land or a threshing machine.

C. What good reasons could his banker advance against jumping at such a golden opportunity to get rich quickly?

The moral of this problem is that every get-rich-quick opportunity is the bait by which some clever manipulator is striving to get-rich-quick himself, without working. The poor old farmer in Missouri might as well have burned up his three-thousand dollar bills. He never got them back and there was not a chance from the first that he would.

NOTES: _____

_____

_____

_____

_____

_____

_____

_____

_____

_____

_____

_____

_____

_____

_____

_____

_____

_____

_____

_____

_____

_____

_____

_____

_____

_____

QUESTIONS ARRANGED FOR INDIVIDUAL AND CLASS STUDY

"I will study and prepare myself and someday my chance will come."

ABRAHAM LINCOLN.

Questions Arranged for Individual and Class Study

The questions which follow emphasize the teachings of each tale and bring out points liable to be overlooked in reading. They are not intended as puzzlers but to develop a deeper insight and understanding.

Personal finances cannot be treated as an exact science. The questions are purposely controversial to encourage discussion and the habit of looking at such matters from all points of view. Therefore, no answers are provided.

Those who wish to reap the greatest possible financial reward from the use of "GOLD AHEAD" are urged to look up the reference to each question and write out their answers in detail with all the examples and logic at their command. File in a loose-leaf container for future reference.

NOTES:

_____

_____

_____

_____

_____

_____

_____

_____

_____

_____

_____

_____

_____

_____

Chapter XIII

THE MAN WHO DESIRED
MUCH GOLD

Study Questions

When a person appears successful, it is natural to think that person is using his head. Financial success may be accidental occasionally but not as a rule. Continued success in any line is the obvious result of good thinking.

When a person, well qualified to be successful and with a healthy ambition to be getting somewhere, finds himself frustrated like Bansir, the cause may be from misfortunes or other reasons. In his case, he gives no suggestion that would point to causes other than those within himself.

Listen to Audio

https://MoreHelp.us/C-13 →

Bansir appears as a hard-working, conscientious artisan. Not quick witted or brilliant, but persevering and capable of good thinking if aroused to the need of doing so. Using the few remarks, he makes about himself as an accurate, though brief, picture of his character, we will, in the questions which follow, bring to the surface those things within himself which were retarding his success. There are many Bansirs in our world today who could and should be doing much better without working one bit harder.

1. Bansir, the chariot builder, is idle through choice and not for lack of work as an unfinished chariot stands in his shop. Write down the cases of one or more people you know upon whom discouragement

acts as a drug, paralyzing both their mental and physical efforts. Or, if you know of no specific cases write your opinions upon such a situation.

2. As he was in such a mood, tell why you think he was justified in taking time out to think instead of trying to forget his troubles by finishing his chariot.

3. Do you feel that by getting orders for more chariots or by charging more for those he made that he could have gotten along in a satisfactory way? Or would a larger volume of money going through his hands just have meant more debts to pay and a continuation upon a slightly larger scale of his hand-to-mouth way of living?

4. In Bansir's dream he pictured himself as being quite affluent. Dream experts claim every dream tells a wish either openly or implied. His dream would plainly indicate a genuine desire for money. Here we have a good artisan with apparently a good business but not making money beyond barest necessities. Write out fully every reason you can think of to explain the causes for such a situation.

5. Bansir said to Kobbi, "I have labored to build the finest chariots any man could make, soft-heartedly hoping someday the Gods would recognize my worthy deeds and bestow upon me great prosperity." Suppose you look within yourself. Do you have some such secret dreams? That someday your ship will come in; that unexpected good fortune will come your way and put you on "easy street"? Write out fully any feelings of this kind you may have no matter how hasy or whether carried over from childhood.

6. Explain why if a person should feel, "I am much too good for this job but someday I am going to be appreciated for my real worth and then, etc.," they could easily coast along under this pleasant illusion

instead of putting forth their best efforts to show themselves suited for a better job?

7. Explain how Bansir may have been so wrapped up in his ambition to build the best chariots that any man could built that he failed to see chariot building as more than actual construction work but instead the means by which Bansir could work out a pleasant and successful life for himself.

8. Kobbi tells his ambition for a larger and finer lyre upon which he could play finer music. Bansir agrees that he should have such an instrument but neither suggests that it might be possible to get one. Neither seems to think they could arrange to get one. Explain how they both fail to face the facts of reality and thus stay on being dreamers.

9. We live in a dual world, a world of mind within us and a world of matter and action on the outside. Within we have imagination and dreams. The practical knowledge we accumulate is a medium through which we can turn our imaginative thoughts into working plans for use in the outer world. Explain how grown men like Bansir and Kobbi could fail to bridge the gap between fanciful ideas and practical working plans.

10. Both Bansir and Kobbi had confidence Arkad would gladly advise them. Arkad, being a very rich man, would of course be frequently approached by people who needed money and asked for help. Explain why Arkad would be much more willing to spend time helping his friends find out how to help themselves than he would to listen to requests for money, even though by nature he was generous and had a great deal of surplus money.

11. A turning point in our lives means that we think or act differently from then on. Explain how the determination of Bansir and Kobbi

to visit Arkad could prove a turning point in their lives and what the results might be.

12. "In those things toward which we exerted our best endeavors we succeeded," Kobbi states. Write out those things in your life toward which you are exerting your best endeavors. Starting at the top according to your amount of interest in each. Then make a corresponding list of the things most important to you for a well rounded and successful life, arrange them according to importance. Then write an explanation of why you should develop the greatest interest in those of most importance. Getting a new understanding, so to speak, on what counts the most in the long run.

13. Kobbi asserted, "With a new understanding we shall find honorable ways to accomplish our desires." State what the words "a new understanding," mean to you. How could you reach a new understanding yourself if you had no such friend as Arkad to whom you could go for enlightenment?

NOTES: _____

_____

_____

_____

_____

_____

_____

_____

_____

_____

_____

_____

_____

Chapter XIV

THE RICHEST MAN IN BABYLON TELLS HIS SYSTEM

Study Questions

This lesson deals with the first basic principle behind success in acquiring money, the right of all persons to keep for themselves a portion of all they earn. Large income is of little advantage except for the temporal pleasures it provides if allowed to go through our hands and leave nothing but memories. A small income judiciously handled may in the end provide much more satisfaction, enjoyment, and worldly possessions than the larger one. As most of us must look to the benefits which an income of moderate proportions can provide, it is essential to our future well-being that we study to become skillful in handling the resources which we have.

1. Explain in more detail the two reasons given by Arkad for the failure of his friends to acquire more than a bare existence from their hard and consistent labors.

Listen to Audio

https://MoreHelp.us/C-14 →

2. From your own experience, can you cite an example of a person coming into sudden and unearned wealth? If so, tell how it seemed to work out, whether to their permanent financial good or otherwise. If you know of no such example, do you agree with Arkad's opinion? Give your reasons.

3. As a youth, Arkad possessed potential possibilities for financial success. Because he succeeded so much better, should we infer that his friends did not possess similar if not equal potential possibilities?

Give your opinion as to what qualities are essential to success with money.

4. As a youth, Arkad was determined to secure a share of the better things of life. Explain the two requisites he considered most essential to doing so.

5. Explain what Arkad meant when he said that learning is of two kinds: "the one kind being the things we learned and knew, and the other being in the training that taught us how to find out what we did not know." Which is the more valuable?

6. What single rule did Algamish, the money lender, give to Arkad as an initial start on the road to wealth? Can you think of a better one? Give reasons.

7. After making his start as Algamish advised, from what other sources than his earnings was Arkad advised to build up his financial surplus? Can you cite examples of the results of compound interest over five years, ten, twenty-five?

8. Just when did Algamish advise Arkad to pay himself? Explain why this was the best time.

9. Arkad explains his first investment and how it turned out. Write out a similar fictitious experience for yourself in which you make an investment that turns out the same way. Select modern people and business conditions, but show how the logical conclusion would be similar.

10. Do the same for his second investment as recommended for his first investment in the preceding question.

11. Why was it wise for Arkad to entrust his savings to the shieldmaker when it was unwise to entrust them to the brickmaker.

12. What was Arkad's next error? Transpose this into a modern example in which the advice of Algamish is used.

13. Explain in detail with reasons the three great fundamentals which Arkad learned and used as the basis of his further successes.

14. Why did Arkad disagree with his friend who said it was just luck that Algamish made of him an heir?

15. Explain your own idea upon will power and just what functions it possesses that will aid in achieving financial success.

16. Do you agree with Arkad that one should not assign oneself difficult, foolish, or impractical tasks? If so, state your reasons.

17. What plan would you recommend to those who desired to get ahead financially and must rely upon their incomes for their start?

18. Did Arkad advise his friends to stint themselves and their families? Do you consider that an average person or family can contract their living expenses 10% without serious inconvenience? What suggestions for so doing can you make.

19. Some of Arkad's questioners realized why Algamish had consistently returned to counsel him. What do you consider the reason or reasons?

20. Just what progress did Arkad need to make before further opportunities opened up for him?

21. Somewhere in his career Arkad made a definite start toward his future successes. At this point he ceased to try merely to make-ends-meet because he had a broader and better vision to guide him. State when you think this occurred and why. Do you feel that you have

arrived at such a point in your career, have passed it, or are still enroute to such a point? Give your reasons.

NOTES: _____

_____

_____

_____

_____

_____

_____

_____

_____

_____

_____

_____

_____

_____

_____

_____

_____

_____

_____

_____

_____

_____

_____

_____

_____

_____

_____

_____

_____

Chapter XV

SEVEN REMEDIES FOR A LEAN PURSE

Study Questions

Being successful in acquiring money is, as the student has already learned, dependent upon keeping for ourselves a definite part of our income. It is also dependent upon our determination to succeed, a determination sufficiently firm and deep rooted that we may overcome the obstacles that are almost certain to confront our determinations. But these are not all the requisites to financial success. In addition, we must have what can be called a financial program or a definite plan of action. Once the cards are in our hands, we must know how to play them to build up the fortunes we desire.

This lesson outlines for us a definite plan of procedure in our personal and financial affairs, by following which we may carry on our successes to wider and more extensive fields. "The Seven Remedies for a Lean Purse" outlined in this lesson will apply to most of us in the broad principles presented, in that they cover the fundamentals of life. They will also apply with slight variations to business institutions and their operation.

Listen to Audio

https://MoreHelp.us/C-15 →

In studying this lesson and in answering the following questions seek for your own use a plan which is practical for you to follow and which will carry you forward to the realization of your own desires and ambitions.

1. The situation of need in which Sargon, King of Babylon, found his people, is similar to the periods of plenty and periods of famine

mentioned in Biblical times. Can you cite parallel periods of modern times? In the face of urgent propaganda to spend freely as a help to national prosperity, do you feel that in times of plenty or even moderate plenty we should make provisions for times ahead which may be more difficult? Give reasons based upon your own interests.

2. Did Arkad advise the men attending his class, earning small amounts, to find more profitable work before endeavoring to get ahead? What were his reasons for the advice he gave them?

3. Arkad affirmed that he had little difficulty in getting along upon nine-tenths of his earnings. Take yourself for example. Write out a budget for yourself which calls for you to get along upon nine-tenths of your present average expenditures.

4. In the Second Remedy, what unusual fact about the inclination of expenditures in proportion to increased income did Arkad point out? Give your reasons for this.

5. Arkad, although he was the richest man in the richest city in the world, admitted his inability to gratify his every desire. Write out a list of your ungratified desires if you have them. Then divide these into three lists under the following classifications, **EASY, DIFFICULT, FANCIFUL.** In the first list include those which are quite within your ability and resources if you decide to gratify them. In the second list put those which call for more money, time, or effort than you can conveniently give to them or which are difficult because of family or other reasons. On the last list include flights of adventure, romance, travel, etc., that are either impractical or unlikely because of lack of money or opportunity.

This is a very worthwhile method of bringing one's desires into the open and releasing one from suppressions. Consider the first list and decide which are really worth gratifying. Then try to do so deliberately, one at a time. Take it easy, as too many at once detracts from the pleasure. Next, consider the second list and make up your mind if any of these would be fully worth the effort required. If so, lay your plans and work for them. For the third list, things that seem impractical, seek a substitute that will gratify your natural longings. In books, we can find travel and adventure which will take us upon thrilling mental journeys to the far corners of the earth. In study classes, we can find mental food and advance ourselves socially and materially. In hobbies, we can find wholesome fascinating outlets for our surplus energies. Don't go through life nursing suppressed desires when there are so many worthwhile things within your reach which you can do.

6. In what ways can you adopt Arkad's plan to eliminate unnecessary expenses to your own expenditures?

7. Do you consider a budget just a useless bother or do you agree with Arkad that it is an ally to defend your most cherished desires against less important demands? Give your reasons.

8. Define the difference between hoarding and building up a fortune. What do you think Arkad would have thought about this question?

9. Define your idea of the most satisfactory form of wealth.

10. Explain more fully the three factors Arkad recommended to be considered when making an investment.

11. When making an investment, do you believe in relying entirely upon your own judgment or should you seek the opinions of others? If others, who?

12. Who can be most benefited by owning their own home? Name the advantages.

13. When a part of one's income is being paid upon a home should

this sum be considered as necessary living expenses or should it be considered as a permanent saving account and therefore a surplus? Or should a part be apportioned to each?

14. Arkad urges financial protection against unexpected need and against want when one is no longer efficient because of advancing years. Explain what opportunities we enjoy now for financial protection which did not exist in his time. How much protection do you feel that you require and how can you secure it?

15. State the methods Arkad used when he was a scribe to increase his earning capacity and how these methods can be applied to yourself.

16. Do you recognize the universal law of change which is always going on in the affairs of men and believe that for the one who prepares himself to be efficient in any line of endeavor a desirable opportunity will open up? Can you cite an example of one who has progressed because he was ready when opportunity came?

17. Review the four things "a man must do if he is to respect himself" and give your reasons for each.

18. Write out the "Seven Remedies" in a condensed form giving a digest of each. Keep or post in a conspicuous place and read often. Make them a part of your daily thinking that they may continually aid YOUR purse to grow fatter and fatter.

NOTES: _____

_____

_____

_____

_____

Chapter XVI

THE GODDESS OF GOOD LUCK

Study Questions

It is quite human to desire to be lucky. To be so in our financial affairs is the theme of this tale. Should there be ways by which we can entice good luck, certainly we wish to learn them? Likewise, if there are ways to ward off bad luck, we would like to know them also.

Listen to Audio

1. Look in your dictionary for the definition of the word "luck." Do the same for "chance." Write out a description of the difference between the two.

https://MoreHelp.us/C-16 →

2. Write a description of any lucky financial happenings that have occurred to you. Explain whether they appeared to be just accidental or whether you were lucky because you took advantage of opportunities which opened up for you.

3. Write a description of any bad luck you have suffered in financial dealings. Explain whether they were because of procrastination, too hasty action, or other reasons for which you might, after thinking it over, consider yourself at fault. Be frank. We all make mistakes. Only the little souls are ashamed to admit theirs.

4. If a Babylonian spent an evening at a gaming table during which he placed 200 bets of one shekel each, according to the laws of average and allowing for the game keeper's profit, would be win or lose? How much?

5. Write out examples giving experiences of yourself or others in playing games of chance, lotteries, the stock market, or anything of this nature, omitting news reports and confining yourself to such things among people you know. Estimate whether the general results were winnings or losses. Try and prove from your actual knowledge whether the occasional winnings are greater than losses.

6. Review the points brought out by the elderly merchant; give the favorable and unfavorable aspects.

7. Would the fact that the plan included the development of the land by supplying it with water make it a better proposition to make money on than if they expected to buy the land and resell it without making improvements? Explain why.

8. Because the young man failed to get into this project when he could have done so, would you consider his failure to be among those who made money out of it, lack of foresight, procrastination, or bad luck? Explain your reasons.

9. Explain what extra advantages there are for those who begin to keep a portion of their incomes at an early age. Name at least three besides those mentioned and write a paragraph upon each.

10. Review the advice of the saddle maker, upon cinching a good bargain with a payment upon account. Can a seller change his mind and legally call off a deal by returning a payment made on account providing the poster is unwilling to give up the deal?

11. Can you recall someone you know who is by nature a procrastinator? Explain whether such a person who puts off from day to day doing things decided upon, is playing safe to make sure of themself or more likely to be carrying on a habit which they have formed. In your opinion is it a habit that prevents progress.

12. Review the opinions of the merchant and Arkad upon the bad results of procrastination.

13. Write a review of the opinion of the cloth weaver given and state why you agree with his conclusions or why you differ with him.

14. Besides being a very rich man, Arkad was a keen observer. Write out more fully his observations upon causes of success or failure as originating within men.

15. Can good luck be enticed to one? Write out a review of what you have learned from this lesson.

16. Napoleon was definitely a man of action. He is reported to have said that he made circumstances. Give example of how circumstances can be made by businessmen to dispose of a surplus lot of coffee.

17. Salesmen generally believe that the law of averages will bring them so many orders if they conscientiously make a certain number of calls upon genuine prospects. Explain how if the law of averages is in your favor, it will work just the opposite from what it does at gambling games where it works against you.

18. From what you have learned from this little journey to the Temple of Learning write out a program for your own future actions which would prove profitable for you to follow—in other words, bring you good luck in the form of logical rewards for your well-planned efforts.

NOTES: _____

_____

_____

Chapter XVII

THE FIVE LAWS OF GOLD

Study Questions

As normal human beings, we possess many intellectual and emotional characteristics which can sway our actions and influence our decisions. The purpose of this lesson is to implant within the student an understanding of a type of temptations which are bound to come to every person traveling upward on the road to greater financial success. Also, to supply them with a method of seeing through these temptations which usually come under one class, opportunities to use one's accumulating capital to make large earnings, in other words, to take short cuts to financial success.

Listen to Audio

https://MoreHelp.us/C-17 →

The broad straight road to success is reasonably safe for the travelers thereon, well policed we might say, by the available knowledge of those who have traveled it and are glad to advise others on their way. But there are innumerable attractive appearing side roads leading off, which are recommended by advisers with self-interests to promote as short cuts to wealth, "get rich quick" trails, actually, along which the brigands and robbers thrive upon the accumulations of the thrifty.

Of course, the student desires to follow the safe road to success and to avoid errors which could cost his savings. The trap of the "get-rich-quick" is always baited with the illusion of big returns for small investments and the "game" the trapper is after is the investor's capital.

The student is urged to memorize **"The Five Laws of Gold"** so that in the future he may wisely judge every opportunity for investing his surplus money and be able to decide upon investments where his capital is safe and can be reclaimed when desired and from which he will receive a fair rate of interest.

1. Nomasir left Babylon and went to a sister city, Nineveh, seeking opportunities. It is an old saying that "Distant fields look greener." In your opinion do you think this idea of going off somewhere to seek opportunity is wise? Or do you feel that the handicap of being a stranger in a strange land, other things being equal, is a serious disadvantage which must be overcome before progress can be made? List the advantages of making such a change. List the advantages of staying where you are known and feel at home.

2. Can you explain just how the men in the caravan with the white horse collaborated with the horse owner in Nineveh to fleece travelers? Is this similar to the methods of modern bunko-men who infest railroads, hotels and busy places, seeking acquaintance with strangers carrying money? Can you cite instances coming to your attention through your acquaintances or from reading of such schemes and how they are worked?

3. Can you give an example of a person buying a business they had no previous training for and trying to make it pay? If so, give facts as to how it panned out. If not, what are your opinions of the chances for success of inexperienced people in new businesses?

4. Do you consider that Nomasir took a long chance in going into business with a man he knew only slightly? Can you cite any examples of such partnerships succeeding? Give your ideas of the kind of partnership combinations that might succeed, supposing the people in question were skillful and experienced either in selling, accounting, advertising, manufacturing management, etc. What are

logical combinations for successful co-operation in running a business and what illogical combinations can you name?

5. Can you give reasons why gold seems to come more readily to those who save a part of their earnings or income than to those who can hardly wait to get it before spending? In other words, why do reasonably provident people usually have money, while the improvident are broke and in more or less financial distress a large part of the time? **The First Law of Gold!**

6. Can you give reasons why gold appears to work so diligently and willingly for some people who not only keep what they have, but enjoy additional revenue from what it earns, while others never derive a satisfactory income from their money? If you believe the way the owners regard their accumulations has something to do with this, explain how. **The Second Law!**

7. The idea of gold clinging to anyone may seem fanciful, yet it has a basis of fact. Can you cite an illustration of a person who has gradually built up a substantial estate without appearing to either have a large income, or, on the other hand, appearing to be penurious or short of money? **The Third Law!**

8. Cite your own experiences with sums of money and state whether it seemed to slip away from you in spite of your desire to keep it. Did you ever try making an investment under the advice of a banker or some party skilled in successfully handling money who was not personally interested in the investment? How far is it safe to be influenced by the salesman? Do you consider that it is his right to present his proposition, but it is your responsibility to prove the safety of the offer before investing? **The Fourth Law!**

9. State, if you can, an example or examples of money "fleeing" from those who were reckless in trusting it to some alluring plan that was to bring very large returns. Can you cite an instance where

someone you know made a winning by investing in cheap promotion stocks? From your own knowledge, do speculative investments in intangible propositions, those not backed by market value properties, offer an assurance of profit without serious risk? **The Fifth Law!**

10. At what point in his career would you say that Nomasir first put his feet on safe financial ground, freed from his impractical ideas about getting rich quick? Explain, why.

11. Would you consider the plan of the slave master to buy enough bronze for the city gates as a sound business proposition? State your reasons.

12. If you are acquainted with a group associated to operate a co-operative saving and investment company such as Nomasir joined, state the advantages in saving, training and earning which they offer to their members. If not acquainted with such a group, state what advantages you feel it would offer to members.

13. Nomasir expresses his opinion of the value of financial wisdom as greater than the value of gold. State your opinion with your reasons.

14. Kalabab states, "Not by some strange magic did I accumulate my wealth." Give your opinion on the harmful influence to individuals of waiting expectantly for "their ship to come in," hoping to find a pot of gold "at the end of the rainbow," and other illusions that someday they will be rich when these ideas are not based upon the results of their own efforts or other tangible propositions of practical value.

15. If you have lost money through an unwise decision or action, do you find the incident inclined to haunt you with unpleasant recollections difficult to forget? If so, write out the incident.

16. Write out a brief statement of any investments or loans you may have made which were unprofitable and state the reasons why. Do the same for profitable loans or investments.

17. Have you ever purposely strengthened your desires as a means of securing their accomplishment? Kalabab states, "In the strength of thine own desires is a magic power." State whether you feel that concentrating your desires upon success in accumulating and handling money will assist you to be more successful and why.

18. Memorize the **"FIVE LAWS OF GOLD."** Do this thoroughly so you can repeat them in sequence and can recite each by number without the sequence. Then cultivate the habit of using these as a yardstick in handling your money as it accumulates. Let them guide you in your decisions. Do not be rushed by decisions based upon desires to take advantage of this or that apparently good opportunity, unless it will stand up under the assay test of merit, under the **"Five Laws of Gold!"**

NOTES: _____

_____

_____

_____

_____

_____

_____

_____

_____

_____

_____

_____

_____

_____

Chapter XVIII

THE GOLD LENDER OF BABYLON

Study Questions

In this tale, we call upon Mathon who makes a business of lending gold for profit. In a confidential talk by him, we are told the essential things to consider in loaning money, if like Mathon, we wish to be able to get it back again.

Mathon was the prototype of the modern banker but without the brass grills and plate glass office partitions. He possessed the same keen knowledge of human capabilities and human weaknesses which the modern banker must have.

Listen to Audio

https://MoreHelp.us/C-18 →

The modern banker may not have Mathon's token chest to guide him, but he has his own training under his superiors coupled with his personal experience to guide him in making safe and profitable loans. When any person remarks, "I would like to ask my banker, but I know what he would say," you may be sure they do not want the cold facts; facts which would tumble their impractical air-castles.

To want to make our own decisions as to what we will do with our own money is natural and desirable. But before making a decision in unfamiliar fields, it is very wise to secure the opinions of experts that our decisions may be as nearly as possible, "fool-proof."

1. Should you come into possession of $5000, as Rodan did, unexpectedly and without any strings attached, what would you do

with it? Write out without restriction the ways you would like to use it. Do not be stingy or let your conscience restrain you. Be guided solely by your desires.

2. Next consider five years ahead. Write out your thoughts, upon what ways you could use it now, what would do you the most-good five years from now. For example, it could be used to go into business, to educate you for a profession, invested in profit earning securities.

3. Explain why it is wiser to make your own plans as to the best disposition of your money instead of simply listening to plans others may put up to you.

4. Give three reasons for not consulting a banker upon any investment plan under consideration.

5. Give three reasons for consulting a banker upon any investment plan under consideration, providing of course you are inexperienced in handling funds for investment.

6. Do you feel that it is taking unfair advantage for a friend or relative to ask one who is building up a reserve through their own frugality and industry, to stake them to go into a business venture without ample security for the safety of the investment? Write out your reasons against such a proposition as that presented to Rodan. Then write out your opinions as to what responsibility he had, if any, to stake his sister and her husband. Before answering these questions, refer to the Problem of the Dentist and his Brother-in-Law in the preceding section.

7. Providing you know examples of inter-family financial transactions, write out a description with the final results. Explain whether favorable or unfavorable and state why.

8. As a rule, would you consider success was surer in business ventures for those who start at the bottom and work up than for those who started out with ample capital and less experience? Consider the handicap of lack of capital for the first and write out your opinions and give your reasons.

9. Here are two types of possible borrowers. Explain which could expect to receive assistance from a banker and why. Also, which could not expect to receive help from a banker and why. "A," A man or woman holding a good position who wished money for education or some constructive purpose, a business man who was making a fair profit and wished money for new equipment or business expansion? "B," A man or woman who, in spite of ability and a fair position was behind with bills and was barely breaking even between his earnings and his expenses.

10. Name the three types of securities upon which Mathon would consider making loans and explain in detail why he considered loans so made to be wise and safe.

11. If you have endorsed notes for others desiring to borrow money from a lending agency, state your experience. Explain how by signing your name upon the back of their notes you make yourself responsible, in case they default in the payments, of paying the entire unpaid balance of the note with interest and, in case of suit against you, to enforce collection, lawyer's fees and court costs. If, having no personal knowledge or experience, consult a business friend and write a paragraph about it. This is a matter to be informed upon. Many well-informed people refuse to make such endorsements. Others do so only after very careful consideration.

12. There is a proverb that if one loans to a friend, they lose both their friend and their money. Write out any experiences you may have had.

13. Review the case of Mathon's two loans to the farmer. Explain why he considered them wise loans. Explain also what is meant by character loans.

14. Review in writing the recommendations made by Mathon for handling the request of Rodan's sister. What other thoughts or suggestions have you to make upon a delicate situation like this. Put yourself in Rodan's place. He was fond of his sister and would like to help her. Yet his gold meant much to him and he desired to keep it. Was the proposed loan of one piece of gold, his savings for one year, too generous an offer? Do you feel that the brother-in-law would have been willing, if employed elsewhere, to have worked for Rodan, evenings and holidays, without pay, just to help him get started?

15. Should the sister become angry at a counter proposal as suggested by Mathon, telling him he was stingy and disloyal to his family, say whether you feel he should weaken and let his inexperienced brother-in-law play storekeeper with the gold which meant so much to him. What should Rodan say to her in defense of his position. Bear in mind that such situations are charged with emotions liable to be difficult to handle.

16. Refer back to the fable of the ass and the ox on. Explain how little practical good the ass was able to do for the ox in spite of his good intentions. Contrast this with the price he paid in humiliation, exhaustion and actual suffering. Write two paragraphs upon the folly of sentimentality in inter-family financial affairs in comparison with treating them from a business basis.

17. After long years of experience, Mathon had decided upon certain definite rules to follow in loaning and collecting money. Write out these rules with your opinions upon them and how you can apply them to guide you in the future.

18. Review the points in Mathon's concluding remarks. Explain how you agree or in what way you differ with him upon his statements in each paragraph.

NOTES: _____

_____

_____

_____

_____

_____

_____

_____

_____

_____

_____

_____

_____

_____

_____

_____

_____

_____

_____

_____

_____

_____

_____

_____

_____

_____

_____

_____

Chapter XIX

THE WALLS OF BABYLON

Study Questions

Walled cities were a common thing in ancient times. In fact, they were still relied upon until not many generations ago.

Such walls expressed man's desire for the safety of himself and the security of his property. In the questions upon this tale will be considered facts upon protection not covered elsewhere.

Listen to Audio

1. The elderly merchant lamented in fear, "My goods they will steal all. My food, they will leave nothing. Etc." Explain what modern provision could he have taken advantage of to protect his goods from theft and fire.

https://MoreHelp.us/C-19 →

2. The woman with a babe also questioned the sergeant about their safety, stating that her husband lay with a fever from his terrible wounds. In case his wounds proved fatal, had he lived in this day, explain what provisions he could have previously made to provide for his wife and their children in case of his death.

3. Explain the two types of life insurance. The one which would have paid the widow a lump sum and the other which would have provided her with an allowance, payable so much each month.

4. Take into consideration the danger of losing her money which would confront a woman inexperienced in handling a sum of money and then say which method would be most likely to take safe care

of her and the children until the latter were old enough to take care of themselves.

5. This nation has experienced several severe panics, which were made more acute by runs upon the banks. Frightened depositors caused the bank to crash. Explain why depositors need no longer fear bank failures for their savings accounts or checking accounts up to certain amounts. Does this apply to all banks, both state and national? Any banker can supply this information.

6. Explain why a savings account is perhaps the most convenient depository for accumulating surpluses.

7. Investigate the savings plan offered by savings and loan associations organized under a special provision of the Federal Government. Explain why money deposited with them is perfectly safe. These all have in their names the words, "Federal Savings and Loan Association."

8. Investigate through your local Post Office what are known as Postal Savings accounts. Write an explanation of their advantage for small investors. All first and second class offices are depositories.

9. Write to the Treasurer of the United States at Washington, D. C., and ask for a pamphlet describing United States Savings Bonds. Give an explanation of their advantages for partial payment investments.

10. If you are an employed person with a large organization, the chances are that a Credit Union exists among the employees. Investigate, and if so, interview the secretary and write a description of the advantages of joining such an organization.

11. Consult a real estate dealer for information as to rates of interest and possible opportunities for safe loans in the form of first

mortgages upon improved real estate. Write out an outline of what you learn.

12. Consider your own affairs, including obligations to those dependent upon you, your properties, funds and investments. Are they all within safely protecting walls? Write out a plan to make you safe from whatever may come.

NOTES: _____

_____

_____

_____

_____

_____

_____

_____

_____

_____

_____

_____

_____

_____

_____

_____

_____

_____

_____

_____

Chapter XX

THE CAMEL TRADER OF BABYLON

Study Questions

In the beginning of this tale, we find Tarkad, a youth of implied good family, adrift, so to speak, like a derelict ship without rudder or sails. He was hungry, broke and shunned by those who knew him.

Much against his desire, he encounters Dabasir, to whom he is already indebted for loans. Dabasir understands this young man. He senses the desperate state of his mind and the serious troubles he is heading for unless something is done about it. Reproaching him for his follies would only increase his defense. Feeding him or loaning additional money would only postpone the inevitable—therefore he tells him the story of his own early life.

Listen to Audio

https://MoreHelp.us/C-20 →

Out of the tale of Dabasir we see developed that transition through which we all must pass before we can achieve what he achieved, the mastery of his own destiny.

1. Tarkad had little desire to meet Dabasir. Explain any reasons you can give why a debtor should avoid creditors. Also, explain the relationship which can exist between debtor and creditor where there would be no sense of shame.

2. If you agree with Dabasir that, "A fortune pursues every man who thinks more of borrowing than of repaying," explain more fully why this should be so. Could a person carry the idea of trying to borrow

so strongly in his minds, he would not give thought to other more desirable ways of meeting pressing needs?

3. The traveler from Urfa told of the piece of stone so thin one might see through it and so colored all the world looked of a different color from what it really was. Give examples showing how this could happen from such causes as being broke, discouraged from loss or disaster, or other causes. Explain how one's ways of thinking could be thrown out of gear for a time.

4. A depressed state of mind can cause lack of interest, discouragement, and inefficiency. Write a paragraph on Tarkad's mental condition explaining why he would continue to sink deeper into his depths of despair until some outside influence awakened his better and finer nature.

5. An investigation in a penitentiary revealed that eighty-five percent of the inmates were there because of crimes committed to obtain money. As a young man, Dabasir had no appreciation of the value of money. Write a review in more detail than given in his tale, of the history of his case which began with thoughtless overbuying upon credit. Then led to borrowing to pay his bills and continued through his break with his wife, his leaving Babylon, and finally ending this phase of his career as a slave in Syria. Trace the initial cause to the ultimate result.

6. Dabasir makes scant mention of his wife, merely that she returned to her father. In lieu of more details, we are justified in thinking that they were equally to blame for the family extravagances which initiated their troubles. Write out your opinion of the probable situation and suggest any actions on her part that would have been wiser than returning to her father.

7. Dabasir worked for two years for caravan traders, but does not mention any thought of applying his earnings upon his debts.

Likewise, when he received his share of the loot from robbing a caravan, he does not mention it. How do you think he felt about his debts during that period? Did he think he could just wash his hands of his responsibility? That they were too large for him to ever do anything about? Or do you think he salved his conscience with the illusion that someday he would strike it rich and make a grand splurge with a return to Babylon to show what a great man they had hounded out of town because of a few small debts?

8. "I was purchased for two pieces of silver," he states in telling how he was sold into slavery. Explain how you think it would make a man feel to be stripped of his clothes and sold for so small a price, sold just like he was a cow or an ass.

9. Through the intercession of Sira, Dabasir was given the position of camel tender by his owner. He thus made use of the few practical things he knew. Many people in times of reverses are forced to turn to any kind of work they can do to support themselves. Often these emergency occupations, however menial they may be considered, prove sound stepping stones to future successes. Give examples of this, or if no actual examples are known, explain how opportunities may be found this way and developed.

10. Sira was quite outspoken to Dabasir. "How can you call yourself a free man when your weakness has brought you to this," she exclaimed. Do you agree or disagree with her that if a man actually does have within him the soul of a free man he can make himself respected in his community in spite of misfortunes? Give your reasons.

11. Do you agree or disagree that merely to have the desire to repay his obligations without doing anything to put these desires into effect proves that his self-respect is gone and within him is the contemptible soul of a slave? Give your reasons.

12. Does it seem to you that Sira laid too much stress upon Dabasir's paying his debts? Could he have regained his self-respect in other ways? Why not by simply making resolutions to do better in the future?

13. Can you give a satisfactory reason why Sira would aid her husband's slave to escape? Did Dabasir arouse her sympathy? Was it because she was resentful at not being her lord's best loved wife?

14. Because Dabasir was willing to accept the offer of Sira to escape and return to Babylon, do you feel that it proved at heart he did have the soul of a free man and not that of a slave? Give your reasons. No blame should be placed upon him for stealing his master's camels. That was simply using his right to escape any way he could from an enforced slavery.

15. Do you agree with Sira that happiness awaits not a runaway wife in foreign lands or anyone else who runs away from their own mistakes or their misdeeds? Explain your reasons.

16. Here we come to the greatest moment in Dabasir's life. Before, he had been dominated by his physical body, his impulses, his appetites, his animal desires. He had been looking at the world from his animal side as through a colored glass. Finally, he was at the end of his rope so far as this side of his character could take him—ready to lie down and die in the desert, a fitting end for a runaway slave. Explain how those super qualities of his mind took control, reproached him for his follies and his weaknesses, and reanimated his worn body with an almost superhuman determination to go back to Babylon and reclaim his lost self-respect.

17. Review Dabasir's explanation of the difference between the soul of a slave and the soul of a free man.

18. Explain how a man like Dabasir who had found his own soul could look with compassion upon Tarkad who was shunned and sneered at by others.

19. "Where the determination is, the way can be found." The way to what for you? Write out not less than a full page upon the advantages of having definite objectives to accomplish, objectives worthy of such a determination as shown by Bansir. Build this about objectives you would like to accomplish yourself.

NOTES: _____

_____

_____

_____

_____

_____

_____

_____

_____

_____

_____

_____

_____

_____

_____

_____

_____

_____

_____

_____

_____

Chapter XXI

THE CLAY TABLETS FROM BABYLON

Study Questions

This lesson considers the question of the obstacles which invariably raise themselves in some way or another between the purposes we wish to accomplish and our means for accomplishing them.

The student who is handicapped by debts that are difficult to liquidate, will see herein a practical plan for solving his particular problem. But that is by no means all that the lesson is meant to teach. There can be innumerable other kinds of obstacles to that success which the student is perfectly competent to achieve.

Listen to Audio

https://MoreHelp.us/C-21 →

Before answering the following questions, the student is urged to take inventory of the obstacles which seem to be retarding his own personal progress to greater financial success. Whatever these obstacles may be, whether debts, responsibility to support others, persons who seem to prevent us from going ahead with our ambitions, or our own personal limitations, environment, or lack of opportunity, bear in mind that success is always the reward for overcoming obstacles in some practical way. Success in getting ahead in our money affairs is the logical result of learning to overcome obstacles and becoming capable of making progress in spite of them.

After visualizing the obstacles which confront you personally, answer the following questions with this in mind. Write out the answers fully and try to find in your answers suggestions for overcoming the obstacles which may be or seem to be confronting you.

1. Give your explanation of the three essentials in the plan which Mathon, the gold lender, suggested to Dabasir whereby he could re-establish himself as a respected citizen of Babylon.

2. Did Mathon's plan take into consideration natural human desires for pleasure and enjoyment or was it a sort of penance for errors? Which should work out to the best advantage in the end?

3. Can you outline a budget for your own earnings that would be consistent with Mathon's plan, allowing you your necessities, shelter, recreation, food, clothing, etc., and still leave for other purposes the proportionate amount which Dabasir was to have to pay off his indebtedness? Try it.

4. In paying off his creditors fairly and honorably, would Dabasir pay an equal sum to each, or would he make a division of the amount available so that each debt, regardless of size would eventually be paid in full in the same number of payments as every other debt? Which would be the fairer way?

5. In this lesson, debts were Dabasir's obstacles. What great truth was it necessary for him to learn before he could overcome his obstacles? Explain how this truth applies to other obstacles.

6. Ahmar, whom Dabasir consider his best friend, reviled him bitterly upon his making the proposition to pay his indebtedness in small payments over a considerable period. Taking for granted that Ahmar was a hard-working young man with a wife who had saved the money by self-denial and thrift, explain why Ahmar should be disgusted with the treatment given him and revile his old friend at the first opportunity.

7. Dabasir's creditors responded differently to his proposed plan of settlement. Do you think their attitude was influenced by their familiarity with his former unreliability? Would a man who had lost his money and gone into debt because of misfortunes other than his own indiscretions have been given more courteous consideration?

8. Explain the factors which kept up his courage and his determination to go through with the plan.

9. When business fell off and his earnings shrunk painfully how did Dabasir get by? Did he incur further debts to keep up a standard of living he and his wife had established for themselves? In an emergency do you feel that their way of meeting a temporary embarrassment was justified and wise?

10. In view of the critical attitude of a number of his creditors at first, can you explain the surprising change when he made the final payment? Why should such a tight old chap as Alkahad offer to loan him money after having had so much difficulty in collecting in previous transactions?

11. Dabasir had no regular income to rely upon. The situation of Professor Shrewsbury was different. Explain which of these two was in the most advantageous position to use the plan and why.

12. Professor Shrewsbury's struggles to get even, had been in vain before he adopted Mathon's plan. He expressed it as a vicious circle. Explain just how this vicious circle worked.

13. Supposing that debt was not the only obstacle to one's advancement or was not even one of them, do you think it practical to prolate one's resources or efforts so as to overcome several obstacles at the same time or would it be wiser to concentrate upon one at a time?

14. What advantages could Shrewsbury offer the merchants to accept the plan? Would any of them have been better off to have refused to accept small payments extending over a long period?

15. Do you think the determination to live upon 70% of their income cost the Shrewsburys severe mental or physical efforts? Did it humiliate them? Was it an interesting experiment to work out, something like playing a puzzling game?

16. In the position of the Shrewsburys with a portion of your income available for a partial payment investment, one upon which you could pay regularly out of each paycheck, what type of investment could you recommend that offered these features? First, the sum paid in, must be absolutely safe from loss. Second, the accumulated sum, must be subject to withdrawal to its full amount. Third, the earnings or interest, must be paid at regular periods in cash, or possibly, if you desired, might be left to accumulate. Look up investments available to the small investor which include these features and other desirable ones.

17. After the Shrewsburys had paid off their indebtedness, what use would you suggest for the 20% of their income they had been using for this purpose? Can you suggest a wiser use than that suggested by the professor?

18. In looking at the teachings of this lesson in their broader aspect, in your opinion, what is the outstanding requisite to overcome obstacles? If you feel that there are several requisites of equal importance, name them and explain your reasons.

NOTES: _____

_____

_____

_____

_____

_____

_____

_____

_____

_____

_____

_____

_____

_____

_____

_____

_____

_____

_____

_____

_____

_____

_____

_____

_____

_____

AHEAD OF YOU
STRETCHES YOUR FUTURE

*"In the strength of thine own desires
is a magic power."*

Chapter XXII

Ahead of You Stretches Your Future

**Ahead of you stretches your future
like a road leading into the distance.**

Ahead of You Stretches Your Future

Ahead, with the fascinating uncertainty of an unknown land lies your future. Waste no idle regrets upon a past that is gone. Look beyond the difficulties and problems of the present. The future is yours and in it you are justified in expecting the realization of your most cherished desires.

Looking ahead into your future and seeing events that are waiting to occur, may seem impossible. Yet, this is what I feel I was permitted to do. Subsequent occurrences bear me out that it actually happened. Certain things which I was permitted to see have come to pass exactly as I foresaw them. Others further ahead, I am looking forward to with full confidence they also will come to pass.

Listen to Audio

https://MoreHelp.us/C-22 →

My most unusual experience occurred in a dream. I dreamt that I was standing in the center of a broad, clay-colored road out in the country. I could see it for a long way as it curved and twisted through a rolling hilly district. As I looked, I gradually became aware that this road represented my life. Back as far as I could see, was my early childhood. The point where I was standing was the present. Each bit of scenery in between was symbolical of the more important happenings of my life, turning to animated pictures of the events as my eyes rested upon them. It was a vivid portrayal of the sequence of assorted experiences which join together to make a life history.

As I stood there a thought came with startling force; how wonderful it would be if I could face about and look ahead into my future as clearly as I was looking back into my past. With a sudden resolve, I turned and looked the other way. Sure enough, the road, my road, continued on far into the distant hills and valleys of the future years.

My first impression was disappointing, or should I say surprising? I, like most folks, expect the future to be quite different from the past and the present. Yet I could see no difference. It was the same identical road continuing ahead with slight change. A few paces forward or backward did not matter.

Gradually the scenes ahead began to shape themselves into readable symbols, similar to the ones behind. With a strange feeling of awe, I realized that, apparently, I was seeing unborn events, events destined to happen to me as I traveled this road ahead. I realized the vision would be fleeting and strained to see as much as I could. Reluctantly I was pulled back to consciousness. Because of my great desire to remember what I had seen, I impressed the pictures vividly upon my mind.

Naturally, the question arises, did these things come to pass?

I can answer truly and without reservation, yes, many of those visions have come to pass and joined the bits of scenery along that portion of my road which lies behind. Something like fifteen years have passed since it was my privilege to look into the future. I have traveled a long way along that road and there is no question but what it is the same road I saw in my dream.

As all who read this whether you realize it or not are following a road, like mine, that leads into a future where you wish desirable things to happen, I am going to tell you some confidential information about the events along my road, things I have learned after following it so long a time.

When I first looked ahead and foresaw so many events pictured as among the major happenings in my future, I was somewhat skeptical. I hardly knew whether to take it for granted some providence, divine or otherwise, ruled my destiny and had ordained these things to come to pass; or whether to take the matter-of-fact viewpoint and wave it all away as just a dream. However, it was not to be forgotten, especially when, as the years rolled by, these prophesied events began to happen.

Naturally, I thought it must be destiny after all. Those events which I most desired to happen were coming true, but as the years passed, I noticed that some which I preferred not to happen did not. Gradually it dawned upon me that through my own desires supported by a definite determination, I could do much to help bring about those things I desired to happen, while even more definitely I could prevent the undesirable from coming to pass.

My original picture proved to be subject to alterations and changes of my own making. Nevertheless, my road ahead is just as real and just as tangible as it always was. I realize I have been most fortunate to have a definite road to follow. It has led me to the fulfillment of many cherished desires. It still guides me ahead. Along my road are other unborn events, the realization of which I greatly desire. Because I know my own ability to aid them to come to pass, I look forward with confidence to their becoming, in due time, realities.

Ahead of YOU stretches YOUR future like a road leading into the distance. Along this road are unborn events, desires you wish to gratify, ambitions you wish to fulfill. Realize your ability to aid them to come to pass. Look forward with confidence to their becoming realities. Be the master of this future of yours, not its slave. Make it the kind of road you wish to follow.

Make it a road that leads to Gold Ahead.

ABOUT THE AUTHOR

Born in Louisiana, Missouri on November 7, 1874 George Samuel Clason became a great American author. After attending the University of Nebraska he served in the United States Army during the Spanish-American War.

Being an entrepreneur, he started two companies, the Clason Map Company of Denver, Colorado and the Clason Publishing Company.

Clason is best known for a series of informational pamphlets on financial matters he authored in 1926. He created characters set in ancient Babylon that taught lessons on financial prosperity. The bankers and insurance companies of his day distributed millions of his pamphlets to their clients to promote saving and investing accounts.

In 1937, Clason first put his words of wisdom together in his book *GOLD AHEAD*. His 2nd edition appeared in 1940. Today, it is better known as *The Richest Man in Babylon*. His writings have fallen into public domain. They have been reproduced numerous times.

George S. Clason passed away on April 5, 1957 leaving this world a better place by helping millions of people financially prosper.

SRAAR Partnership
Website: https://MoreHelp.us/C-40
Email: SRAAR@EinsteinThinkers.com
1310 Wilkinson Drive
Plant City, FL, USA 33566

QR Codes sends you to the chapter-by chapter professional narration of Steve Hoover.

Series: Read and Listen by QR Codes

Made in the USA
Columbia, SC
17 December 2022

74350729R10130